Also available at all good book stores

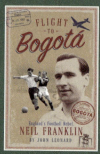

9781785316548

9781785316760

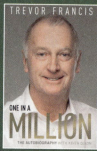

9781785314995

9781785316685

9781785316807

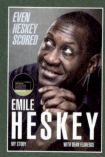

9781785315008

9781785316333

9781785317255

9781785315510

First and Last

How I Made European History With Hibs

First and Last

How I Made European History With Hibs

JACKIE
PLENDERLEITH

With
Tom Maxwell

First published by Pitch Publishing, 2021

Pitch Publishing
A2 Yeoman Gate
Yeoman Way
Worthing
Sussex
BN13 3QZ
www.pitchpublishing.co.uk
info@pitchpublishing.co.uk

A CIP catalogue record is available for this book
from the British Library.

ISBN 978 1 78531 989 1

Typesetting and origination by Pitch Publishing
Printed and bound in India by Replika Press Pvt. Ltd.

Contents

For Mum and Dad – *Jackie Plenderleith*

For Sabrina – *Tom Maxwell*

Foreword

I WAS a young player at Manchester City when Jackie Plenderleith signed in the summer of 1960, ostensibly to replace the mighty Dave Ewing at the heart of the City defence. The only similarities between the two of them, however, were that they were both from Scotland and they both played at centre-half, but in a completely different way.

'Big Dave', from Perthshire, was rough, tough and seemingly hewn from granite. He was loud and ebullient, an old-fashioned 'stopper' who was loved by all City fans for his enthusiasm and his commitment to the cause. In came Jackie, signed from Hibernian, a Scotland Under-23 and future full international. He was smooth, cool and a picture of urbanity who preferred to defend with anticipation instead of decapitation. A tidy and accurate passer of the ball with good control, but the polar opposite of what City fans had become accustomed to. This included Jackie's pre-match, ball-juggling routine on the pitch, which wouldn't have looked out of place in a travelling circus.

It was something totally different. The fans loved to see a player performing a few tricks with the ball because, in those days, before the game defenders would simply stand 30 yards apart and belt the ball to each other, while the forwards would gather around the edge of the penalty area firing shots past their own goalkeeper into the net. So Jackie was ahead of his time, really, but his ball-juggling exploits weren't confined to the football pitch. The snooker room, upstairs at Maine Road and after training, was the place to see Jackie perfecting his favourite party trick of tossing a billiard ball high into the air before catching it neatly on the back of his neck. It was a dangerous thing to do but he never failed to catch it – don't try this at home!

I made my reserve team debut at Stoke City, playing alongside Jackie. He had been absent from the first team for quite a long spell and his future at the club at this point seemed a little uncertain. As we got back into the dressing room at Stoke's old Victoria Ground after the game, however, he still went out of his way to tell me how well he thought I had played in what I am sure for him was a meaningless 4-1 win but for me was just the opposite.

As fate would decree, Jackie and I both left Manchester City on the same day in 1963 and, a few weeks later, I bumped into him on Oxford Road. I was pleased to see him. He was always great to me and showed a genuine interest in the youngsters. 'Are you joining Lincoln City?' he asked. I said that I was. 'I want to wish you the very best of luck.' And then he was gone, back to Scotland and the next phase of his life.

As someone who spent most of his football career in the reserves, I can only imagine what it was like for Jackie – when he was barely 17 – to be playing regularly in the Hibs first team alongside such club legends as Gordon Smith, Lawrie

Reilly and Eddie Turnbull, let alone to play in the very first staging of the European Cup. Jackie is a good man with a great story.

Fred Eyre, author of *Kicked into Touch*

Prologue

'IT'S JUST a joke.' That's how Alan Hardaker, secretary of the
Football League, had apparently described this new competition
– the European Champions Clubs' Cup – to the men in charge
at Chelsea. Why would you want to send your boys overseas
when there are perfectly good trophies up for grabs at home? In
the end, the forward-thinking Yorkshireman persuaded the 1955
English champions to send their apologies to the organisers,
despite having initially accepted the invitation. They'd leave
that continental nonsense to those Real Madrid and AC Milan
fellows, thank you very much.

Maybe Mr Hardaker was erring on the side of caution after
what had happened to England's national team five years earlier.
After scoffing from afar at the first three World Cups, England
finally entered the tournament in Brazil in 1950, only to be sent
packing by a bunch of part-timers from the United States. Not
that the men in charge of the Scottish FA were shining beacons
of globalism. Ahead of the same tournament, they threw their
toys out of the international football pram and refused to travel
to South America for what would have been Scotland's first
appearance at the World Cup. Why? Because England had

beaten them to top spot in the Home Nations Championship. But hindsight is a wonderful thing.

Hibernian weren't champions of Scotland when we were invited to take part in the very first staging of the European Cup – a competition now known to millions around the world as the Champions League. To paraphrase that old joke about Ringo Starr not even being the best drummer in The Beatles, we weren't even the best team in Scotland. In fact, we weren't even the runners-up, having finished the 1954/55 season behind Aberdeen, Celtic, Rangers and Hearts. We'd actually finished up closer on points to Motherwell in 15th place than we had to the Dons in first.

From what I could understand at the time, our invitation had less to do with our performances, or even the championship wins in the glory days of the Famous Five a few seasons earlier, and more to do with the fact we'd recently installed top-of-the-range floodlights at our home ground of Easter Road. So that's how we found ourselves, the fifth best team in Scotland, playing a midweek game in a half-empty stadium nearly 800 miles from home in the pissing rain. I wiped the mud from my face for the umpteenth time and found it hard to argue with Mr Hardaker's assessment. Maybe we would've been better off staying at home and concentrating on the domestic trophies.

We were in the city of Essen, West Germany. I'd never heard of it. But then, I wasn't what you'd call worldly. I was just a 17-year-old boy from a small mining town in Lanarkshire. Although I'd been in the first team for nearly a year, I was still the youngest player in the Hibs ranks and – prior to this match – I'd rarely set foot in England, let alone Germany. I'd boarded an aeroplane for the first time and flown there alongside legendary figures like Eddie Turnbull, Lawrie Reilly and Gordon Smith – still one of the greatest footballers to play the game. But while I appreciated being in a team of such huge names, the fact I would be playing against a side boasting players such as Helmut 'Der Boss' Rahn – scorer of two goals in the World Cup Final a year earlier – was something that was lost on me.

Like the majority of people in Scotland at that time, I'd never even watched a World Cup match. My family didn't own a television and I certainly had no idea of the significance of the Miracle of Bern, where Rahn helped the underdogs defeat the mighty Hungary and announce the Germans as an international football force to be reckoned with. All I knew about the country was that it was a hell of a long way to go to play in the mud and pouring rain in front of 5,000 spectators – I could've done that back in Holytown.

I know this might sound like I'm trying to play things down, but did it dawn on me at the time that I was making history as a member of the first British side to compete in the European Cup? Not a chance. Like so many firsts, the significance of the occasion has only grown as the years have passed. A man in his 80s views things a little differently to a boy who's not yet 18. If the European Cup, the Champions League, or whatever they're calling it, is still going in 100 years' time, long after I'm gone, nothing will ever change the fact that I was there when it all began.

In the 66 years since that inaugural season, when Real Madrid won the first of their 13 titles to date, I've sat back and watched some truly spectacular players grace the competition, including Cruyff, Zidane, Ronaldo (both the Brazilian and the Portuguese), Messi, Gerrard, van Basten and Bale, not to mention giants of defence such as Maldini, Baresi and Beckenbauer. They all made their marks in the competition for different reasons but, even if it was only because they were born too late, none of them were there at the start. Would I swap that distinction for scoring a spectacular overhead winner in the final? I'm not sure I would go that far.

But when I talk about the importance of that first season growing with time, it's now more significant to me than ever. After the death of Tommy Preston in 2015, the 17-year-old who lined up in the rain all those years ago is the last of those historic Hibbies standing. Whatever else I did in my career, including playing in front of nearly 100,000 fans in a cup final, lining up alongside Denis Law for Manchester City, plying my trade on another continent, and playing for my country, it's in a green and white shirt that I was lucky enough to make history. I stuck my football boots in the wet cement of the world's greatest club competition and – alongside the rest of those Easter Road players – that's where they'll stay for as long as football is played. Strange to think, then, that there was only one club I ever wanted to play for when I was a kid, and it certainly wasn't Hibs.

1

Jack the Lad

I'M THE first to admit that Willie Woodburn probably isn't everyone's idea of a football idol, certainly not in the mould of Pelé or Diego Maradona. First of all, he was a centre-half or 'pivot', which is rarely considered the most glamorous position – unfairly, in my opinion. Second, he had the unfortunate distinction of being the last British player to receive a lifetime ban for something he'd done on a football pitch. Or, to be more specific, for headbutting a Stirling Albion player. But Willie Woodburn was my hero. Not for the headbutt, I hasten to add. I just loved the way he played the game: dominant in the air, uncompromising in the tackle, yet skilful with the ball and a terrific reader of the game. The Scotland defender was one of the main reasons I grew up supporting Rangers.

We didn't have much money when I was a boy but, when we could afford it, I'd go on the supporters' bus to Ibrox and watch in awe as Woodburn would put some of the country's top strikers firmly in his pocket. He won three titles in a row with Rangers in the late 1940s, at the time when football was starting to occupy almost my every waking thought. His team-mate George Young was another hero, and I was also a big fan of Bobby Evans at Celtic.

I remember telling a friend that I wanted to be a central defender, just like Willie Woodburn. He looked at me as though I'd taken a blow to the head. I didn't care. Because of Woodburn, central defence was the only position I ever wanted to play in. Years later, I nearly became another of Woodburn's victims. I was doing my apprenticeship as a joiner while playing for Hibs. One day I was up a ladder, two stories up, repairing a window in the centre of Edinburgh when I heard someone shouting my name.

'Jackie! Jackie! How are you doing?'

I looked down and nearly lost my balance when I saw the great Willie Woodburn smiling up at me. After retiring from football (his 'lifetime' ban was revoked three years later when he was 37 and past it), he'd become a sports reporter for the *News of the World*. Now here he was, the man I'd idolised from the terracing, coming to interview *me*. I couldn't believe it, but I did wonder if he'd have received a lifetime ban from journalism if I'd ended up in a heap on the pavement. Having said that, maybe it would've been worth it if he'd signed my casts.

I was born John Boyd Plenderleith in Bellshill Maternity Hospital, in North Lanarkshire, on 6 October 1937. The hospital was demolished in 2003 to make way for housing. As far as I know, there are no plans for a blue plaque bearing my name! Situated about ten miles south-east of Glasgow city centre, Bellshill is a town that – even now – has a population of only 20,000, but, over the years, it's produced more than its fair share of professional footballers. Among the best known are Billy McNeill, who captained Celtic's 'Lisbon Lions' to become the first British team to win the European Cup; Hughie Gallacher, one of Scotland's most prolific marksmen and one of the 1928 'Wembley Wizards'; Rangers and Scotland star Ally McCoist; Brian McClair, who won an impressive haul of trophies during his time at Celtic and then Manchester United; and Phil O'Donnell, the Motherwell captain who died tragically at the age of 35 after collapsing during a game.

But perhaps no Bellshill soccer alumnus is more famous than Sir Matt Busby, the Manchester United manager who nearly perished alongside eight of his 'Babes' in Munich and rebuilt the club to become European champions ten years later. Busby was considered a visionary of English football, his side following in Hibs' footsteps by entering the European Cup in 1956, the year after our run to the semi-final, and reaching the same stage of the competition. He once said that at Manchester United they would strive for perfection, but failing that would have to settle for excellence. I'm not sure if I ever had such lofty ambitions when I was a schoolboy, but I always knew I wanted to be a professional footballer.

Although born in Bellshill, I grew up in a street called O'Wood Avenue in nearby Holytown. There must have been something in the water in North Lanarkshire because this was a village very close to where the free-scoring brothers Joe and Gerry Baker were from. Both would become my team-mates, Joe at Hibs and Gerry at Manchester City. Another footballer from Holytown was Harry McShane. Although a league title winner with Manchester United in 1952, his fame has been somewhat eclipsed by that of his actor son, Ian, better known to millions as television's *Lovejoy* and, more recently, Winston in the *John Wick* movies. There was nothing so slick – or violent – at the pictures as *John Wick* when I was growing up, but I was an avid cinema-goer and I loved Westerns in particular. Aside from playing football, there was nothing I liked more than settling down with a choc-ice and watching stars like Alan Ladd in *Shane*, Gary Cooper in *High Noon* and Jimmy Stewart in *Winchester '73*. Even today, I love sitting down with a Cornetto and watching some of these old movies.

Holytown wasn't exactly the type of place where you'd find gunslingers, but it was a little rough around the edges in those days. One of my earliest memories, it must have been around 1942, is of watching a succession of military vehicles thundering past our tenement building. I wondered where they were headed, but at four or five I had no understanding of the devastating toll the war was taking on Scots both at home and abroad. Being a coal miner, my dad John didn't go to war. Instead, he worked hard on the home front, down the pits of Auchengeich, Thankerton and Cardowan. It was an incredibly dangerous profession, a fact we were reminded of several years later, in 1959, when 47 men were killed in a fire at Auchengeich. Remembering the sight of my dad coming home day after day, exhausted and covered from head to toe in coal dust, made me thankful that my ability with a football was one of the things that spared me from following him down the mineshaft. It was probably what spurred me on to achieve my ambition. An amateur goalkeeper, my dad recognised that I had talent and did more than anyone to encourage me. He was incredibly supportive and rarely missed a game when I was at Hibs.

Like a lot of miners, who spent so much of their time without seeing natural light, my dad was a keen gardener and I helped him from a young age. In my early teens, I kept a couple of Angora rabbits as well as pigeons, something I'm still passionate about today. My dad met my mum, Annie, in Bellshill, at what people of a certain generation affectionately called 'the dancin'. Annie was actually a moniker. Mum's real name was Ona Balavage. Her parents had come over to Scotland from Lithuania, and they weren't alone. It was estimated that, at that time, North Lanarkshire was home to around 10,000 Lithuanians and, even today, Bellshill is where you'll find the Scottish Lithuanian Social Club. A small and tough woman, she would chase me through the house with a brush if I was being stupid – and not just when I was a schoolboy. But she was also very loving and supportive, not to mention a tremendous cook. I know lots of boys will say this, but no matter how far I travelled and how many hotels I stayed in during my career, I never tasted anything as good as the soup that Mum made.

The eldest of four, I was followed by my brother Robert, my sister Anne and then, finally, by Richard. Mum always wanted a daughter and I suppose with Anne it was a case of third time lucky. Robert would later become a professional footballer with Montrose. Richard didn't show the same interest in the game and, on one occasion, I walked out the back door to find my kid brother burying my football medals in the garden! I used to spend quite a bit of time at a pond known as 'The Big O', named after O'Wood Avenue. This is where me and my pals would spend many happy hours, finding tadpoles in the summer and going skating in the winter.

I was also in the Boys' Brigade from a young age and even played the drums in their pipe band. I was privileged to attend the centenary celebrations of the 1st Holytown/12th Motherwell Boys' Brigade in 2014. As well as it being a good laugh, I found the sense of discipline and camaraderie I learned at the Boys' Brigade useful when it came to my National Service and, of course, to football. I started playing at Holytown Primary and continued at Bellshill Academy. My friends and I would be out in the yard every breaktime and lunchtime, squeezing in as much football as we could before the referee's whistle – or, more accurately, the school bell – would interrupt us and we were forced back into the dreariness of the classroom. Outside school, come rain, shine, sleet or snow, my friends and I would play for hours on end. If the ball we were playing with burst, we'd get old newspapers and tie them up with string for a makeshift replacement, anything to keep the game going. It's amazing how much your ball control improves when you're forced to play with a pair of rolled-up socks. Personally, I think they should include it in the coaching manuals.

But whatever the ball was made of, I liked scoring goals and I think I was pretty good in any position. However, it was at centre-half that I enjoyed most success. My best friend when I was growing up was a lad called Davie French, who was a very fast centre-forward and would often benefit from my ability to pick him out with a long pass. I used to tell him that whenever I got the ball, he should start his run and I would kick it over the defenders' heads. I accept it wasn't the kind of pure football that would've won us admiration from people like Matt Busby, but we scored quite a few goals that way. We used to practise our close control when we were on our way to play football in the park. We'd leave the house and play keepie-ups, headers and kicking the ball between us without it once touching the ground. We must've got pretty good at this because the park was a decent distance, but it helped that there weren't as many cars going around back then.

My ability was first noticed by the schoolmaster son of Peter Bennie – a director with nearby Airdrieonians – while playing in the playground, something that ultimately led to me to enjoy two years of training alongside the Diamonds at Broomfield Park. My performances at Bellshill Academy led to appearances for the Lanarkshire schools team, but one of the greatest thrills came in 1951 when Holytown took on Chapelhall in the final of the oldest school football tournament in the world. Established in 1886, the Airdrie Schools Cup was a big deal. Although now at Bellshill Academy, I had been invited back as captain and a crowd of almost 9,000 – nearly double the attendance of my European Cup bow – watched us win 3-1 at Broomfield. Afterwards, we were serenaded through the streets by a pipe band as hundreds of people cheered us on to our bus. Victory in the competition was becoming something of a Plenderleith tradition. My uncle Dick, my dad's brother, had won the trophy when he was at school and, in 1956, my brother Robert was also on the winning side. The adulation we received following our cup victory was an amazing feeling and one I thought I'd like to get used to. The best way to do that, I figured, was to play as much football as I possibly could.

One of my early newspaper interviews described me as a 'glutton for the game'. I always laugh when I hear about modern footballers and managers moaning about fixture congestion when they've got to play four games in the space of 11 days. I'm an old man now, so I don't mind sounding like one when I say that these footballers don't know they're born. At one point, I used to think nothing of playing three full games on a Saturday: for the Boys' Brigade, for Holytown and for Bellshill Academy. I would be absolutely exhausted by the time I collapsed into bed, but I'd be up early and raring to go again the next morning. Even an early injury didn't keep me out of the game for long. I was playing in a match for Bellshill Academy against Larkhall Academy when I went in for a 50-50 challenge. It was actually more like a 30-70, but I was never one to shirk a tackle. On this occasion, shirking would probably have been the best option. There was a sickening crunch and, while the other lad sprang to his feet, I felt a sharp pain and lay on the ground clutching my leg. The referee came over and asked me what the problem was.

'I think I've broken my leg,' I wailed.

The referee looked sceptical and put his hands on his hips. 'Don't be daft,' he barked. 'Now get on your feet and stop holding up the game.'

I got on my feet but continued to hold up the game because, two seconds later, I had collapsed in a heap and had to be stretchered off.

Luckily, the break wasn't too bad and I was only out for a month or so. I was soon back to playing several matches a week, and no match gave me more pride than the one I played on 2 May 1952, when I was named captain of the Scotland Schoolboys Under-14 team to take on Northern Ireland at Grosvenor Park in Belfast. We won 5-2 – a scoreline that I'd enjoy again with the senior team a few years later. One of the things that gave me most pleasure was the way I was described in the match programme as 'a tower of strength in defence and attack'. I read and re-read that passage so many times I could have recited it by heart.

But while my football reports were something to be proud of, the same couldn't be said of my reports at school. Now firmly convinced I could make it as a professional, I took the decision to leave when I turned 15 that October. My parents, understandably, weren't thrilled, but they knew my heart wasn't in my studies. I remember that I had enjoyed some classes, most notably French, but the only thing I was really interested in was *le foot*. After leaving school, I signed for Ferndale Athletic. I was at the Glasgow juvenile side for about a year, but things could sometimes get a bit hairy on the terraces. Despite the close proximity to the punch-ups, however, I was still desperate to play the game for a living and Ferndale was certainly a good place to toughen a young lad up.

I knew that few people could become rich playing football – how times change – but I could make a decent living from it if I made it to the top. My dad, however, was a realist. He knew that it was important to become useful with my hands as well as with my feet, and he encouraged me to learn a trade. I had made a decent job of the rabbit hutch in the back garden, and so I began my joinery apprenticeship at a local firm called Aitken's. Aside from the long hours and the occasional splinter, it was something I really enjoyed, but it helped that nearly all of the chat was about football. Most of the lads were Airdrie fans, of course, so I wisely kept my support for Rangers hidden under a bushel.

I was very lucky that Airdrieonians let me train at Broomfield, where I learned a lot from people like trainer Billy Steel, the former Derby County, Dundee and Scotland forward. Taking lessons from a man who had represented his country on 30 occasions, including when he scored in a memorable 3-1 win at Wembley, was invaluable. Training at Broomfield also saved me having to travel into Glasgow to drill with the rest of the Ferndale players, but I think there was always an assumption that I would ultimately sign for Airdrie. There was no doubt they were a decent side, but at that time they were still in the old 'B' Division and I wanted to keep my options open. I was starting to attract attention and, while playing for Ferndale, I was spotted by somebody from Doncaster Rovers and invited down to Yorkshire by their manager, Peter Doherty. Rovers were enjoying their loftiest ever status under the former Ireland international, playing in the old English Second Division. I also travelled down for a trial at Preston North End, home of the great Tom Finney, but I was terrified because I found myself playing against a lot of older boys who towered over me. It was like Land of the Giants.

Ultimately, I decided I wanted to pursue a football career in Scotland. I was familiar with the football scene up here and, still a young lad, I didn't feel ready to leave my own country. As I approached my 16th birthday and I started to get more and more attention from scouts and from local newspapers, there was no shortage of Scottish clubs showing an interest. All I had to do was choose. Growing up is all about learning to make big decisions, and this was surely one of the biggest I'd ever have to make.

2

If the Boots Fit

SO HOW did I end up at Easter Road? Don't get me wrong, like everyone else I was a huge admirer of the Famous Five and of the way the Edinburgh side played football. Not that I had ever seen them in the flesh. Most of what I knew about them came from match reports in the newspaper. Whenever I got the chance to steal a look at the sports section, there was no escaping the exploits of Gordon Smith, Bobby Johnstone, Lawrie Reilly, Eddie Turnbull and Willie Ormond. They were legends in their own lifetimes and are – quite rightly – still regarded as one of the greatest, if not *the* greatest, forward lines in history. One can only imagine what damage they might have been able to inflict had Scottish selectors had the courage to play all five of them together – even once – for the national side.

During my formative football years, the feted forwards led Hibs to consecutive league championships and they were just 17 minutes from leading them to a third, only for Rangers to sneak the 1953 title on goal average. Considering that, in Hibs' entire history, the club have won the championship on only four occasions, with all bar Johnstone involved in the title win of

1948, it's no wonder this group of players are still being talked about so many years later, not to mention having the North Stand at Easter Road renamed in their honour. But even considering the prospect of playing alongside these Hibs heroes, those who knew my affinity for Rangers wondered why, when I had men from Ibrox chapping at my door – as well as representatives from Aberdeen, Airdrie, Motherwell and Newcastle United, among others – I decided to head to the east coast.

Part of it, as that most well-worn of football clichés goes, was about playing percentages. My dad, who although not better at football than me was certainly better at sums, told me that I'd probably have a better chance of making the first team in Leith than I would in Govan. And if I had the chance again, I'd make the same decision. I had been training with Airdrie since I won the Schools Cup with Holytown and the assumption was that, when I finished my education, I would become a permanent fixture at Broomhall Park.

But I knew Hibs were serious about signing me when, in April 1953, they invited me to watch Scotland take on England at Wembley. Unfortunately, neither my dad nor I were able to get time off work and it meant we missed an absolute classic. Lawrie Reilly, my future team-mate, got two goals, the second one a 92nd-minute equaliser after being played through by Bobby Johnstone. The strike gave Scotland a share of the British Home Championship and cemented Lawrie's lifelong nickname: Last Minute Reilly. While obviously disappointed not to make it down to Wembley, I was able to travel the more manageable distance to Hampden to watch Hibs play Celtic in the final of the Coronation Cup on 20 May 1953. As the name suggests, the tournament was part of the celebrations to mark Princess Elizabeth's accession to the throne. It consisted of four English teams: Arsenal, Tottenham Hotspur, Manchester United and Newcastle United; and four Scottish teams: Celtic, Rangers, Aberdeen and Hibs, who were invited as the reigning league champions.

Celtic had seen off Arsenal and Manchester United to book their place in the final, while – following a replay – Hibs had beaten Spurs and gone on to thrash Newcastle 4-0 in the last four. And although Celtic – with future European Cup-winning manager Jock Stein at centre-half – took the unofficial title of 'Champions of Britain' after a 2-0 win, it was an incredible thrill to watch the team that wanted my signature playing in front of nearly 120,000 spectators at the national stadium. I'd been to Ibrox on the supporters' bus three or four times to see Rangers, but I'd never experienced anything quite like this. It's not called the 'Hampden Roar' for nothing and watching players like Smith and Reilly in the flesh for the first time is something I'll never forget. And there was an even greater thrill to come when my father and I were invited to go to meet the players afterwards. I'd love to be able to say that I played it cool, but what 15-year-old boy wouldn't be awestruck when coming face-to-face with some of the most famous footballers in the world? I was so excited that I could barely drink my lemonade.

If I'd been swithering about whether to join Hibs prior to that match, there was absolutely no doubt in my mind afterwards. Of course, I still had a soft spot for Rangers – they were my boyhood club – but, from that moment on, I didn't want to be anything but a Hibby. Hugh Shaw, who had guided

Hibs to three Scottish championships following the death of Willie McCartney midway through the 1947/48 season, came to our house to sign me on a provisional basis (basically the footballing equivalent of putting dibs on me) until I turned 17. People were thrilled when they heard I'd be signing for Hibs, with the notable exception of my boss at Aitken's. An ardent Airdrieonians fan, he'd read in the newspaper that the Edinburgh club were going to sign me and he told me that, if I wanted to play for Hibs, I could bloody well piss off to Easter Road and find myself another job. Come to think of it, he may not have put it so politely.

That was a bit of a blow but, when Hugh heard about my predicament, he was happy to sweeten the deal. The club would set me up with a firm in Edinburgh, so I could continue my joinery apprenticeship. My boss there, at least, would welcome a new Hibs player with open arms – his brother was Harry Swan, the club's chairman. As was usual with a lot of new Easter Road signings, I was farmed out to Armadale Thistle in West Lothian to get some more experience under my belt. The appropriately named George Farm, the Scotland goalkeeper, and Jimmy Leadbetter, who would go on to win the English First Division under Alf Ramsey at Ipswich Town, were among the players who had started out at Armadale, so I knew the Junior club was of a decent standard. The feeling was clearly mutual with an Armadale coach telling the local paper that I was 'the best thing that had happened to junior football for ages'.

When it came to training with the Hibs first team in Edinburgh, it was a bit of a hard slog at first – even for me. I would get up around six o'clock every morning and catch the seven o'clock bus through to Edinburgh. I'd train with Hibs for a couple of hours and then go to work in town for the rest of the day before travelling home. When I was a bit more established and started getting the train, I didn't travel alone. It's difficult to imagine now, given the heated nature of some of the Edinburgh derbies over the years, but I usually made the journey from Holytown Station with a couple of Hearts players: winger Johnny Hamilton and full-back John Thomson, who I played with at Armadale.

And yes, I know we were all called John, but you've got to remember that this wasn't long after the war, and first names were still being tightly rationed. As teenagers wearing tracksuits and with stars in our eyes we probably looked a bit out of place among the suits and ties on the daily commute, but we didn't care. Despite playing for different sides, all three of us had a common dream of being professional footballers. If that didn't motivate you to get out of bed in the morning, then I don't know what would. Johnny certainly had a powerful motivation. Like his Hearts team-mate, Alex Young, he was serving his apprenticeship at a colliery. He would eventually score more than 150 goals while in Gorgie.

Like Johnny, I found the early starts, the training and the work tiring, but I couldn't have been happier. Although I continued to impress for Armadale and in training at Easter Road, there was still a nagging doubt that, for whatever reason, Hibs might not offer me a full contract when I turned 17. I spent my last night as a 16-year-old feeling anxious, but I got the best birthday present I could possibly have asked for when I reported to training the following morning: a piece of paper to confirm that John Plenderleith was officially a Hibs player, on the princely sum of £5 a week.

Even better was that I didn't have long to wait to make my first-team debut – only a fortnight, in fact. For someone who had been so keen to play my football in Scotland, it was ironic that I should end up making my Hibs bow in Reading, coming on for the second half in a Wednesday evening friendly at Elm Park. Like Hibs, Third Division Reading had only recently installed floodlights, beating Racing Club de Paris 3-0 on my birthday in a match that was broadcast live on the BBC and watched by millions throughout Europe. Just two days before our match against the English side, the official opening of Easter Road's own floodlights took place with a friendly against Hearts. Although not the first club in Scotland to install floodlights, ours were seen as the brightest and best – something that would stand us in good stead the following season. But despite playing my part in a 2-2 draw in Berkshire, I was quite prepared to accept that I might have to wait a little longer before I made my competitive debut.

While it was true that the team hadn't made the best of starts to the 1954/55 season, losing three and drawing one of their opening four league games, things had started to improve with successive victories over Queen of the South and Raith Rovers. If things continued this way, I might conceivably have to wait until the end of the season, or even the season after that, to play a game in anger. Many footballers will tell you that there's an element of luck when it comes to getting your big break in the first team. Some might benefit from an injury, others from a suspension. Personally, I had John Buchanan to thank. Three days after the match at Reading, the Clyde striker scored a hat-trick in a 6-3 hammering of Hibs at Shawfield.

Even by the less impressive standards of the previous season, when Hibs had finished fifth, the result came as a shock. Hibs supporters had been used to their club being the ones who dished out drubbings like that. Not since the early years of the war – in 1940 – had they shipped half a dozen goals. With Hibs sitting on three points and in 12th place, the 'A' Division table made grim reading for Hugh Shaw. He was forced to shuffle his pack and, for the match against Kilmarnock at Easter Road the following Saturday, he took a gamble on a lad just three weeks into his 18th year. Out of the Hibs defence came George Boyle and Jimmy 'Tiger' Thomson and in came me and – much to my surprise – Eddie Turnbull, who normally played at inside-left but had switched to the half-back line for a friendly draw against Newcastle a few days earlier. It was by no means the end of the road for young Jimmy, who I'd later appear alongside in our European Cup run.

Goalkeeper Tommy Younger, who had won two titles with Hibs and would go on to represent Scotland at the 1958 World Cup, had requested a transfer following the match at Clyde, and was replaced in between the sticks by Donald Hamilton. Centre-forward Lawrie Reilly had returned to the Hibs line-up for the first time that season in the match against Clyde, having recovered from a bout of pleurisy and pneumonia which kept him out of the World Cup. Before that, he'd gone on strike due to the fact that Gordon Smith had been awarded a testimonial and he hadn't. Having finally made his long-awaited return to the football field, Lawrie did what he did best – putting the ball in the back of the net – but the haemorrhaging of goals at the other end was something that clearly needed addressing. And so the Clyde match marked the Famous Five's penultimate appearance together as a forward line, as 31-year-old Eddie – who was taking his turn as captain for the season – made the shift into defence to face Kilmarnock, with Tommy Preston taking his position at inside-left. Tommy had been filling in for Lawrie at centre-forward with spectacular results, so Hugh Shaw was keen to keep him in the side.

I'm sometimes asked why, despite the hundreds of games I played in my career, I never managed to do what a defender like Sergio Ramos, the long-serving Real Madrid centre-back, has done on a regular basis. At the time of writing the controversial Spaniard has scored 126 goals during his career (including more than 20 at international level), which is exactly 126 more goals than I ever scored. But, aside from the natural scorer's instinct, there's a major difference between the two of us – Ramos never had to play alongside Eddie Turnbull. As a 17-year-old, if you're screamed at by Eddie on more than one occasion to 'get the fuck back in defence where you belong' every time you venture over the halfway line, hanging back becomes second nature. I think Eddie ingrained in me an almost Pavlovian response to curb my striking instincts. Even several years later while playing in South Africa, my ears would start to ring for fear of a Turnbull bollocking if I ventured too far upfield. That's my excuse, anyway, and I'm sticking to it.

And so with a pre-match warning to keep things tight, I made my competitive debut for Hibs against Kilmarnock at Easter Road on 30 October 1954. I was so excited that I even treated myself to a new pair of bootlaces to mark the occasion – a tradition that I'd continue for the rest of my career. But even in front of nearly 30,000 fans I didn't feel overawed, possibly because I knew we couldn't fare much worse than we had against Clyde. Nevertheless, I was determined to do my bit and hopefully get my career off to a winning start. It very nearly didn't. Losing 2-1 with two minutes to go, we were awarded a penalty, which Eddie – as was usually the case – dispatched with ease. We were relieved just to get a point, but we then made sure of the win a minute later when Willie Ormond scored his second of the game.

The full-time whistle went on my first official match as a Hibs player. It was certainly a dramatic introduction. I felt I'd acquitted myself well and I got plenty of encouragement and pats on the back from my team-mates. One newspaper headline even claimed that I 'stole the show' – no mean feat when you're playing in the same side as Eddie and company. And it meant a great deal to me when Lawrie said, 'Most centre-halves in those days just hoofed the ball up the park, but that was never Jackie's game. He was a footballer from the moment he stepped into the team.'

Aside from being among the first players to compete in Europe, the thing I'm asked about most often is what it was like to play with the Famous Five. I can honestly say it was a privilege. As individual players they were superb, but as a forward line they were peerless and – Eddie's on-field expletives aside – they were all very friendly. They were always quick to offer me help and advice, especially Gordon Smith. I was going through a period where I felt I hadn't been playing particularly well and I asked him what he thought I could do about it. He told me I was a great centre-half and told me just to keep attacking the ball. He was right. What some people might not realise, however, is that – quite naturally – the attention the quintet received from the media and the supporters sometimes led to a bit of a 'them and us' mentality among the players at Easter Road.

Any time we went to a dinner or function, the five of them would all sit together and it created a bit of resentment among some of the defenders. After all, we played 11-a-side football, not five-a-side. These feelings would occasionally boil over in training, especially when we'd play forwards against defenders. On more than one occasion, the tensions led to fisticuffs and the entire squad being sent home early. None of this bothered me, however. I was just glad to be at Hibs and having players of the calibre of Reilly, Ormond, Smith, Johnstone and Turnbull on your side far outweighed any of the jealousy it sometimes caused, especially as they were still capable of scoring goals for fun.

The victory over Kilmarnock was the beginning of a roll. It was followed by successive victories over Stirling, Motherwell, Dundee, East Fife and St Mirren. In the 4-1 win over Motherwell, it was suggested that I knew how to 'use the heid'. This wasn't in a Willie Woodburn sense and laying it on another player, but that I wasn't one for hefty clearances. Instead, I tried to play measured passes to start up attacks. I had certainly become a more cultured player since my school and junior days when I used to belt the ball up to my mate Davie, who sadly hadn't made the grade during his own trial at Easter Road. I was gutted for my best friend, but I was determined to seize my chance. After being on the winning side in my first six matches and with Hibs having climbed up to fourth place in the table, the arrogance of youth had allowed me to think that this professional football lark was actually easier than it looked. But then, as it always does, the honeymoon came to an end. In my case, it was a 5-0 thrashing at home to Celtic. Under the captaincy of Jock Stein, the man who would turn them into European champions in 1967, Celtic did most of their damage with three goals in 14 second-half minutes.

Although my first experience of playing against the Old Firm was one to forget, I only had to wait a fortnight for my second, and it was one to remember for all the right reasons. On 25 December, we beat Rangers 2-1 in front of 43,000 delirious supporters at Easter Road. I also found myself up against another future European competition winner. On the field that day, in his final season as a player, was future Ibrox manager Willie Waddell, who would lead Rangers to European Cup Winners' Cup glory in 1972. And no, I didn't have any mixed feelings about beating the club I supported as a child. If someone had told me that I'd be playing against Rangers on Christmas Day, when boys not much younger than me were busy unwrapping their new train sets, then I'd have thought you still believed in Santa Claus. I was in dreamland.

I can't be bothered with these players who don't celebrate when they score against their old clubs. You've got to remember who's paying your wages and show a bit of respect for your supporters. I'm not saying you should run the length of the pitch to celebrate in front of the opposition fans, like Emmanuel Adebayor so infamously did for Manchester City against

Arsenal, but don't keep your arms by your sides and pretend you're not happy to have scored a goal. Some of us would have given their right leg to do that! But while Christmas 1954 was something for Hibs and their fans to celebrate, we had a far from happy new year, losing 5-1 to Hearts in front of nearly 50,000 at Tynecastle on 1 January.

This was my first introduction to that other celebrated Edinburgh forward line, the 'Terrible Trio' of Alfie Conn, Willie Bauld and Jimmy Wardhaugh, all of whom were on the scoresheet that day. Hearts were league runners-up the previous season and in October 1954 they had won their first major trophy in nearly half a century when they beat Motherwell in the League Cup Final. It was obvious that the balance of footballing power in Edinburgh – at least for now – was well and truly shifting to the west of the capital. Helped by players like Dave Mackay, John Cumming and, of course, the Terrible Trio, Tommy Walker's side would go on to win seven trophies in the space of nine years.

Our 3-2 defeat at Clyde in front of 15,000 fans on 29 January turned out to be an historic occasion, when the Famous Five appeared as a forward line for the 187th and final time. And the changing of the Auld Reekie guard continued in February 1955 when Hearts went one better than their league win and beat us 5-0 in the Scottish Cup, a match I was lucky enough to miss. I returned the following week in a 3-0 win over Kilmarnock on 12 February, which was Bobby Johnstone's final game for Hibs before signing for Manchester City. Coincidentally, it was also Gordon's 600th appearance for the club and Lawrie marked the occasion with yet another hat-trick. Bobby would return a few seasons later, but that was the last time the Famous Five ever played together.

Results over the rest of the season were mixed, with the high point being a 2-1 win over Celtic at Easter Road. Just as they'd done the season before I joined, we eventually finished fifth, this time behind Aberdeen who secured their first title, Celtic, Rangers and Hearts. My own season finished prematurely, although only just, as I managed to break my foot against Queen of the South in the penultimate match. It was a disappointing – not to mention painful – end to my first campaign. I was probably too preoccupied with my foot but it later dawned on me that, with Bobby's departure, I had been a first-hand witness to the end of an incredible era. And I didn't know it then but the following season would see Hibs at the forefront of a brave new one.

3

The Great Unknown

IN DECEMBER 1954, not long after we had been hammered 5-0 by Celtic, Wolverhampton Wanderers were being crowned champions of the world. The honour hadn't been given in any official capacity, but rather by the *Daily Mail*, which saw the defeat of Honved in a friendly at Molineux as definitive proof that English football was the best on the planet. Beating the Hungarian champions – featuring six members of the 'Magnificent Magyars' side that humiliated England 7-1 a few months earlier – certainly wasn't to be sniffed at but, for one Frenchman at least, Billy Wright's Wolves still had a lot to prove.

Gabriel Hanot, a former international and the editor of sports newspaper *L'Equipe*, wrote, 'Before we declare that Wolverhampton are invincible, let them go to Moscow and Budapest. And there are other internationally renowned clubs: Milan and Real Madrid to name but two. A club world championship, or at least a European one – larger, more meaningful and more prestigious than the Mitropa Cup [which featured only central and eastern European teams] and more original than a competition for national teams – should be launched.'

And they didn't waste any time. Backed by Jacques Goddet, *L'Equipe's* owner, and journalists Jacques de Ryswick and Jacques Ferran (first names were apparently being rationed in France, too), the idea for a 16-team continental competition was taken both to FIFA, the world governing body, and to the newly founded European body, UEFA. It was presented to UEFA's very first congress in Vienna in March 1955. *L'Equipe* then invited 18 clubs to a meeting in Paris. Among the representatives of the 16 clubs to attend the French capital was none other than Harry Swan, the chairman of Hibs. One of the main points agreed at that meeting was that this should be a competition open only to the league winners of each nation – but *only* once its inaugural season had been completed and the 16 invited teams, including Hibs, had taken part.

As so, just four months later, my team-mates and I – playing for the fifth-best club in Scotland – found ourselves in West Germany for the first staging of the Coupe des Clubs Champions Européens, or the European Champion Clubs' Cup. For all we knew back then, this might have been both the first *and* last season of the new competition. Although given the blessing of FIFA on 8 May – the tenth anniversary of the Allies' victory in Europe – it was on the proviso that the participating clubs must first have the blessing of their respective national associations.

The English FA, for one, felt that the new tournament was a distraction from the domestic trophies and encouraged the 1955 league champions, Chelsea, to stay at home. This was despite their name being on the original fixture list when it was announced in July. Not that this should have come as a surprise. Twenty-five years earlier, FIFA had been unable to scrape together 16 teams for the first World Cup with the four Home Nations among those to decline the invitation and Scotland not competing until 1954. Only 13 teams went to Brazil in the end, with the four representatives from Europe only agreeing to make the long trip to South America following a personal intervention from Jules Rimet, the FIFA president.

With England unwilling to send their top side and, just like the World Cup, scepticism rife, the organisers had no choice but to be selective if they wanted their new European club tournament to be a success. Just like today, where the Champions League can be won by a team which finishes outside the top three in their own country, the title of the competition was something of a misnomer. As much as we wanted to be, Hibs weren't the Scottish champions. If the league season had been a race then we hadn't even made it on to the podium, yet we were the ones invited to dine at Europe's top table. So, why had we been approached? Well, there was no doubt that we were a well-known team on the continent, and even further afield. There was a reason our striking quintet, now a quartet, were called 'famous'. We also had the best floodlights in the country, something that would be essential for hosting midweek matches with evening kick-offs.

There was the fact that, under Harry Swan, Hibs had already shown a desire to see the world and to try new things. This was best illustrated when just two years earlier they'd accepted an invitation – as Scottish champions – to go to Brazil to compete in what the Brazilian FA had termed a World

Club Championship. Some have since claimed that seeing Hibs perform in this tournament had a profound effect on the way the Brazilian national team played their football. There might be some truth in that, but for Hibs it was very much a case of 'have floodlights, will travel'. Finally, and it would seem remiss not to mention it, there was the not insignificant fact that Harry Swan happened to be president of the Scottish Football Association – and chair of its Executive Committee – at the time.

Despite all the success (including European glory in the Cup Winners' Cup) they later enjoyed under Alex Ferguson, many Aberdeen fans are still left wondering what might have been had their team – who had become Scottish champions for the first time in 1955 – been the ones to compete in that first European Cup. And, having lived in the Granite City for the last 42 years, I've had more than one punter take great pleasure in debating with me on this point. I can't say I entirely blame them. I'm not sure how Hibs supporters would have felt had they been champions and the SFA, with the Aberdeen chairman as president, had allowed fifth-place Aberdeen to compete in a new competition called the European Club Champions' Cup. Aberdeen would have to wait 12 years before playing their first match in Europe and 25 years before competing in the European Cup. Back in 1955, however, there was talk that the club themselves weren't keen to take part, being well-known opponents of matches taking place under floodlights.

Although we'd been one of the clubs first sounded out by the organisers, the *Daily Mirror* also had its doubts about our right to compete, quipping that the organisers 'must have been working with a 1952 yearbook'. On 24 June the newspaper wrote, 'As president of the Association [Harry Swan] naturally looks after the interests of all member clubs. In his tenure of office he has done that nobly. But as chairman of Hibernian FC he is in quite a spot. Back from Paris, where the European Federation has been meeting, comes news that the new club championship, the first Continental international club competition of all time, will start at the end of this year with 16 teams from different countries taking part. Hibernian were invited by the French newspaper sponsors when the scheme was contemplated and the club accepted, as representing Scotland. But the Europe Cup is now an official affair, and the Scottish FA must now sponsor the team which will represent the country. Can Harry possibly let Hibernian be that team?'

The answer, as history and I can attest, was yes. After all, it would be rude to accept an invitation to a party only to then send your apologies, as Chelsea were encouraged to do. Besides, of the 16 teams taking part, only seven – Aarhus (Denmark), AC Milan (Italy), Anderlecht (Belgium), Djurgårdens (Sweden), Real Madrid (Spain), Stade Reims (France), and Rot-Weiss Essen (West Germany) – were national champions.

In addition to Hibs, the other teams were Gwardia Warsaw (who had finished fourth in Ekstraklasa, Poland's national league); Partizan Belgrade (fifth in Yugoslavia); PSV Eindhoven (third in the Dutch championship play-off); Rapid Vienna (third in the Austrian league); Servette (sixth in Switzerland); Sporting Lisbon (third in Portugal); and MTK Budapest, the runners-up in Hungary. Completing the line-up were the footballing oddity of FC Saarbrücken who, although finishing third in

West Germany's Oberliga Südwest (south-west premier league), belonged to a state that had been under French occupation since the end of the Second World War.

While the Allied occupation of West Germany officially ended in May 1955, the Saar Protectorate didn't rejoin West Germany until 1957. Their 'national' team, comprised almost entirely of Saarbrücken players, had impressed when beating Norway in the 1954 World Cup qualifiers, hence the club's invitation to compete at the European Cup. Their right to take part was helped quite possibly by the fact it was a French-organised competition.

Whatever the reason for the invitation, Saarbrücken, like Hibs, were honoured to be taking part, with our manager Hugh Shaw saying, 'The feeling is one of enormous pride that Hibernian are embracing a wonderfully exciting new European competition. My chairman, Mr Swan, has long since advocated a tournament between European club sides. As for some of the debate about which teams should or shouldn't play in the new competition, I leave that to others to speculate. The politics of football doesn't interest me.'

As a teenager who hadn't even played a full season as a professional, I was even less interested in politics – football or otherwise. Having broken my foot towards the end of the previous campaign, I was busy concentrating on getting myself fit for the season ahead. I didn't even hear about our date with European destiny until I reported for pre-season training. Even if the club had wanted to give us a heads-up they'd have had to send a telegram because we didn't have a phone in the house.

When I did find out about the new competition we'd be playing in I was excited, but I was nervous too. Most of the players didn't bat an eyelid at the thought of heading to West Germany in September. The majority of them were, as Eddie Turnbull put it, 'seasoned travellers', but the same couldn't be said for me. Up to that point, Reading was the furthest I'd ever been, and I certainly wouldn't have been able to point to Essen on a map. We'd be flying over there and I had never been on a plane. That didn't bother me so much as the fact I'd also need to get myself a passport.

* * *

Come August, I was looking forward to starting my first full season at Easter Road. And before heading off to the continent, I had another competition in which to make my debut – the League Cup. The group games would all be played before the league campaign got under way, with the quarter-finals taking place in September and the semi-finals and final being played in October.

We'd been drawn in Group 3 alongside Clyde, Dunfermline and – wouldn't you know it – Aberdeen, who would visit Easter Road for our first match on 13 August. Now being managed by Davie Shaw after Dave Halliday had taken over at Leicester City, the Dons were a team we'd be utterly sick of the sight of within a few weeks. We were now, of course, without Bobby Johnstone, with the long-serving Bobby Combe, who also ran a grocer's shop on Leith Walk, taking his place in attack.

But while the Famous Five were no more, myself, Jimmy Thomson and Tommy Preston had already formed a slightly less famous three. At 17, 21 and 22 respectively, we were the youngest half-back line in the country, with the brilliantly versatile Tommy happy to trade in his shooting boots in order to stay in the side. We lost our first match 1-0 against Aberdeen to a Paddy Buckley goal but could have snatched a draw had Eddie, who had resumed his rightful role up front, not missed a penalty. We followed the defeat with a 2-2 draw against Clyde, before Eddie made up for his penalty miss against Aberdeen by putting away two spot-kicks in a 3-1 win over Dunfermline.

Gordon really opened my eyes when we travelled up to Aberdeen, not just with his skill on the pitch but with the contents of his wallet. We were at the train station and arranging ourselves into taxis to get to Pittodrie. Gordon hailed one and said, 'I'll get this.' With that, he took out his wallet, which contained a wad of ten bob notes about two inches thick. I nearly died when I saw it and asked Gordon if he was planning to buy the taxi. When we got to the ground, Lawrie put us ahead just before half-time but Buckley and then – with two minutes to go – Joe O'Neill condemned us to yet another defeat.

This effectively ended our League Cup hopes, but it was a tight game and we liked to think we would fare better in two weeks' time, when we were due back in Aberdeen for our first league match. If we thought losing to them twice in the League Cup was bad, however, what happened next was the stuff of nightmares. The frighteningly quick Buckley, a Scotland international and a key member of the title-winning side – not to mention also being a Hibs supporter from Leith – scored against us for the fourth game in a row, this time helping himself to a hat-trick in a 6-2 win for Aberdeen. It was our fifth straight loss to the Dons over two seasons and, the way we were feeling as we trudged off the pitch at Pittodrie, we were beginning to wonder if we'd ever beat them again.

We were shellshocked and the *Daily Mirror*, again, seemed to take great delight in our current shortcomings. Under the headline 'Hibs aren't good enough', the paper said the result was proof that the wrong team had been given the honour of representing Scotland in the new European competition. 'The lesson is clear,' it wrote. 'Any Europe Cup games for the future should be given to the national champions.'

Given what took place in Germany, it was clear that I wasn't the only one in the team who felt galvanised by what happened in Aberdeen, or by what we read in the newspapers. You could say it gave us a granite-like resolve. For me personally, it wasn't much fun to be on the end of a defeat like that, and Hugh Shaw let us know it. The last time Hibs had conceded six goals, almost a year earlier, it led to wholesale changes in defence and also to my own debut. Now that I was in the side, I was damned if I was going to be out of it again so quickly. I told Hugh that I would try twice as hard and, if I did have any shortcomings at Pittodrie, I would make sure they weren't on display in Germany.

Rot-Weiss Essen, who had beaten West Germany's World Cup-winning captain Fritz Walter's Kaiserslautern to their domestic championship, was a tough draw. Actually, draw is probably the wrong word. There had been no glitzy three-hour television extravaganza of ex-footballers in velvet suits and sporting fixed grins pulling names at random out of a hat. For the first and only time in the history of the tournament, the ties had been chosen by the organisers. It's unthinkable now, but it takes time for competitions to settle on formats and rules. If any team ever thinks they get a raw deal, then spare a thought for Cologne, who in 1965 went out to Liverpool on the toss of a coin. The rumour was that if that year's final between Inter Milan and Benfica couldn't be decided on the pitch, respective captains Armando Picchi and Mário Coluna would have to play 'rock paper scissors' in order to choose a winner.

And so the day before our match in Germany, armed with a small suitcase and gripping my new passport tightly, we headed to Edinburgh Airport from where we'd fly to Düsseldorf via London. Having never flown before, I wasn't sure what to expect. The aeroplane looked very small from the terminal and, after walking across the tarmac with the other players and the coaching staff, I realised it was also very small viewed from close up. To me it looked more like a Spitfire than a passenger plane and, on board, the walk from the tail towards the cockpit was so steep that I had to hold on to the seats. The flight itself didn't bother me, however, as I was too excited about the adventure ahead. As we boarded the second plane in London, we waved to photographers from the steps. None of them, or any of their reporter colleagues, would be accompanying us to Germany – something that rankled with Harry Swan for years afterwards.

As well as talking about the match on the way over, there was also a fair bit of chat about the country we were heading to. It was, after all, only a decade since the end of the Second World War. In their autobiographies, both Lawrie and Eddie talk about there being an element of grudge about the match. Eddie had lost friends in the war, while several of our team-mates – including Tommy Preston, whose father had been killed at Normandy – had lost members of their family in the conflict.

I could understand their feelings, but I think a mixture of youth and the fact my dad was a coal miner meant that, to me, it was only a football match and, despite our poor recent form, it was a football match we were eminently capable of winning. Our chances were boosted when we learned that Essen would be without their star player, Helmut Rahn, through injury. Known as 'Der Boss', Rahn had scored the winning goal when West Germany had shocked favourites Hungary in the World Cup Final just over a year earlier. While narrowing our odds, it was a pity not to get the chance to lock horns with such a star name. Any footballer will tell you they want to pit themselves against the best.

Not that Essen's starting XI were in any way short of talent. Goalkeeper Fritz Herkenrath, for example, was on the verge of winning his first cap, and would line up for West Germany throughout the 1958 World Cup. My opposite number Heinz Wewers was already an established international, while fellow defenders Walter Zastrau and Willi Köchling would also be called up by *Die Mannschaft*. With plenty of talent on both sides, it was a shame that only 5,000 – less than a third of the crowd who'd watched us get thumped at Pittodrie at the weekend – turned up to witness this moment of football history for both nations.

* * *

Georg-Melches-Stadion, which had been refurbished following heavy bomb damage during the war, had a capacity of 30,000 and had been hailed the 'German Highbury'. And more than 76,000 were in Hanover to watch Essen claim their first – and only – German championship with a thrilling 4-3 over Kaiserslautern three months earlier. The apathy might have been down to a combination of it being a Wednesday-night kick-off and a new and unfamiliar competition. The pouring rain didn't help either. Besides, we knew we shouldn't take it personally. Just under a week earlier, in the third game of the competition, only 7,000 watched Real Madrid's 2-0 victory over Servette in Geneva, gates that today's Real B team would be ashamed of. And the following week, barely 3,500 would be in Stockholm to see Djurgårdens draw 0-0 with Gwardia Warsaw.

And looking more closely at those who had bothered to venture out into the rain, it soon became clear that there weren't many German fans among them. The crowd was, in fact, comprised mostly of British soldiers who were based nearby. I doubt many of them would ordinarily have supported Hibs, or Scotland for that matter, but they were more than happy to cheer on any British side against the Germans. And what they lacked in numbers they more than made up for in noise, especially when Eddie pounced on a loose ball on 35 minutes to become the first British player to score in European competition.

The appalling conditions didn't affect our play, and they didn't seem to bother the fans either, although that may have had something to do with the local booze. I was less concerned by the rain than I was by the mud, which clung to my boots and meant I felt at times like I was trying to run in wet cement. With scant regard for the feelings of our kit man, at one point

I slid in for a tackle and wondered if I was ever going to stop. We hoped we could hold on to our lead as half-time approached and Lawrie made sure of it with our second goal on 44 minutes, running from the halfway line and beating several Germans before slipping it past the goalkeeper. We picked up where we left off after the break with Eddie getting his second on 53 minutes and, with under ten minutes left, Willie Ormond completed the rout.

Hugh Shaw said afterwards that it was 'maybe just as well' that we stopped at four, given how jolly our new fans were at the full-time whistle. It wasn't only our forwards who'd played a blinder. Everyone in the team had performed brilliantly. Not only had we become the first British side to play a competitive game in Europe, but we'd also picked up the first win and, of particular pride to me, we'd kept the first clean sheet. We were helped by our full-back pairing of 22-year-old John Higgins and seasoned campaigner Jock Paterson, along with Tommy Younger, Scotland's number one, in goal. Hugh said afterwards that we'd beaten the Germans 'at their own game', while Gordon Smith, who was captain for the season, said, 'We deserved it. We've been playing good football in all our games and it just had to come off some time. This was it.'

Essen's manager Fritz Szepan didn't see it that way. The only reason we'd won, he claimed, was because – being from Scotland – we were more accustomed to playing in rain. That was right up there with Alex Ferguson's 'wrong shirts' and Kenny Dalglish's 'bouncy balls' in the dodgy excuse stakes. We flew back to Edinburgh the following afternoon and, given our result in Essen, we were disappointed not to win away at Clyde on the Saturday with the Bully Wee scoring a late penalty in a 2-2 draw. It was a punishing schedule but a couple of days later, on Monday 19 September, we gave our supporters an Edinburgh holiday they'd never forget when we welcomed Matt Busby's young Manchester United side to Easter Road. We showed that we really were a force to be reckoned with by beating the Busby Babes 5-0.

* * *

But it's still hard for me to think about that amazing win without it being tempered by the fact that, less than two and half years later, three of the men I lined up against that night – Roger Byrne, Mark Jones (my opposite number), and Tommy Taylor – would be among the eight United players to perish on a frozen Munich runway while on European Cup duty. Another two, Johnny Berry and Jackie Blanchflower, never played football again.

Blissfully ignorant of what was to come, we kept the momentum going into our next league match, a particularly satisfying 1-0 victory over Hearts at Tynecastle. I played one of my best early games for Hibs and managed to keep Alex Young – aka 'The Golden Vision' – quiet. 'Jackie couldn't just defend,' said Lawrie later, 'he was also a classy and cultured player which was very unusual for a centre-half in those days.'

Jimmy Mulkerrin, a 23-year-old squad player, delighted the travelling fans by scoring a close-range winner in the 85th minute and he followed this up with another goal in a 2-1 win over Kilmarnock. Just before our return leg against Essen at Easter Road, we enjoyed another spectacular victory over English opposition on Monday, 3 October, with a 4-0 win at Preston North End. The great thing about those floodlight matches was the chance to come up against greats of the English game that we wouldn't ordinarily encounter. A couple of seasons later, I had the pleasure of playing against John Charles – sometimes centre-forward, sometimes centre-half – of Leeds United. It was shortly before the Welshman, known as the Gentle Giant, signed for Juventus, where he would become the Italian side's greatest ever overseas player. He gave me the most uncomfortable match of my career up to that point, and it was possibly never topped. He really was the complete footballer, but the match ended up in a 4-4 draw.

It was coming up to the first anniversary of my debut – a fact I was reminded of when I turned 18. We were certainly going into our second European game on a better run of form than when going into our first, but we hadn't reckoned on the weather again playing a part. This time it was fog. And Phileas Fogg in the case of Tommy Younger, Lawrie and Gordon, who were busy putting Jules Verne's globetrotting hero to shame while on international duty with Scotland.

After travelling home with us the day after the Preston game, they sailed to Belfast for a British Championship match that weekend. After Lawrie scored – and had his knee badly clobbered – in Scotland's 2-1 defeat, they sailed home, before immediately flying to Copenhagen to represent the Scottish League against the Danish League. We later received word that Lawrie's knee had swollen up badly and his place would be taken by Hearts' Alfie Conn, with the injury also ruling him out of the second leg against Essen. The problem happened during a collision with Northern Ireland goalkeeper Norman Uprichard and would eventually curtail Lawrie's illustrious career.

Mulkerrin would play at centre-forward against the Germans, but we were confident that, with a 'fast car' waiting for them at Prestwick Airport the following day, Gordon and Tommy could still be at Easter Road in time for the 8.15pm kick-off. The morning after the Scottish League's 4-0 win, the Scotland players flew to London and it was there, waiting for a connecting flight to Prestwick, that the fog rolled in and left our men stranded. Two more – relatively – young squad players were drafted in at the last minute. Willie Adams, a 19-year-old goalkeeper signed from Ormiston, made his one and only appearance for Hibs. Willie, who I believe is still with us, was walking down Easter Road when he received a tap on the shoulder and was told that, rather than being a spectator, he had to get changed, sharpish.

Jock Buchanan, meanwhile, had famously only just finished his dinner when he got the call to make the mad dash to the stadium. Not that being full of mince and tatties did him any harm, putting the ball in the net after only five minutes to score the first goal on British soil in European competition. Even missing three of our key players and the return of Franz Islacker – scorer of a hat-trick in the German championship final – wasn't enough to stop us reaching the quarter-finals, although Islacker did briefly manage to stop me in my tracks when one of his ferocious shots knocked me out cold. In stark contrast to Essen, a crowd of 30,000 were in Edinburgh to watch us draw 1-1 and subsequently join Real Madrid, Partisan Belgrade,

Rapid Vienna, Stade Reims, AC Milan, MTK Budapest and Djurgårdens in the next round. We were in some esteemed company and couldn't wait to see which exotic city we'd be visiting next.

4

Home from Home

AS SCOTLAND'S largest city, Glasgow has seen plenty of memorable European football matches over the years. Two examples that spring immediately to mind were played at Hampden Park: the European Cup Final of 1960, when Ferenc Puskás and Alfredo Di Stéfano ran riot in Real Madrid's 7-3 victory over Eintracht Frankfurt; and the 1970 semi-final of the same competition, when Jock Stein's Celtic beat Don Revie's Leeds United in front of 136,000 fans.

This was the first of many European matches to be dubbed the 'Battle of Britain', with Rangers defeating Leeds on another thrilling occasion at Ibrox in 1992 – the first season of the Champions League. Ibrox was also the scene of Rangers' victory over the great Bayern Munich side of Franz Beckenbauer, Sepp Maier and Gerd Müller in the 1972 Cup Winners' Cup, while Celtic fans will long cherish the night in 2012 when their team sent Lionel Messi's Barcelona packing. And, naturally, who will ever forget the Champions League Final of 2002, when Zinedine Zidane's sublime volley against Bayer Leverkusen at Hampden secured a ninth title for Real Madrid?

But the first European match to be played in Glasgow wasn't at Hampden, Celtic Park or at Ibrox. It was played in November 1955 in the rather more modest surroundings of Firhill Stadium, home of Partick Thistle and, for one night only, the home of Swedish champions Djurgårdens. After rain and fog had played a part in our first-round matches, this time it was the freezing winter conditions of our opponents' homeland that had led to a switch in venue.

Even though the Stockholm side had international ice hockey star Sven Johansson (who was later known as Sven Tumba) in their ranks, not even they fancied playing on a frozen surface. None of us could deny that it was more convenient for us to drive the short distance along the A8 than it was to fly to Stockholm, but I couldn't help but feel a tad disappointed that I wouldn't be adding a Swedish stamp to my new passport. For the Swedes, the expense of travelling to Scotland for their 'home' leg was more than made up for by the fact that they didn't need to pay for the away team's accommodation, while they also got to keep the gate receipts, with the 30,000 in attendance comprised mostly of Hibs fans who'd journeyed from Edinburgh. But the tie that saw the unique sight of a Swedish team playing a side from Edinburgh in Glasgow could have been very different. If the English FA hadn't decided at the 11th hour to lean on their league champions and encouraged them to withdraw from the new competition, there was every chance that our quarter-final would have seen us paired with Ted Drake's Chelsea. In the end, football fans in the UK would have to wait another 15 years to watch European football's first Battle of Britain. Chelsea's late withdrawal saw them replaced by Gwardia Warsaw, who were subsequently knocked out in the first round by Djurgårdens.

But I think that, given how we were playing against English opposition in our Floodlight Challenge matches, we would have had a decent chance against the Blues. In the run-up to the match at Firhill, we followed up our impressive victories over Manchester United and Preston North End with home and away wins over Newcastle, the FA Cup holders. We also beat FA Cup runners-up Manchester City at Easter Road, with their impressive side featuring not only Footballer of the Year Don Revie but also inside-right Bobby Johnstone. It had been less than a year since his £22,000 transfer from Hibs, and 'Nicker' was given a warm welcome by the Easter Road faithful on his return. Bobby may have scored at Wembley but his old pals Lawrie Reilly and Willie Ormond combined to make sure he left his old stamping ground empty-handed.

Our match at home to Newcastle was a bit of a strange affair. With fog rolling in from the Firth of Forth making visibility poor, the players – and the 16,000-strong crowd – were at one point under the impression that the match had been abandoned. The players shook hands only to learn that management and officials had actually agreed to an extended break and then call it a day after 70 minutes. The one advantage of playing in an unofficial league, as one newspaper put it, was that we were able to make up the rules as we went along.

Things were going well in the league too, with a run of five wins and a draw since our 1-1 draw with Rot-Weiss Essen. Our form clearly had our next European Cup opponents worried. A few days before the first leg, Sigvard Bergh, Djurgårdens's president, had made the long journey to Palmerston Park in Dumfries to see what he could learn about from our match against Queen of the South. Whatever information he gleaned during our 3-1 win, Bergh's presence in the stands was a sure sign that the Swedes were taking the challenge seriously. Although competitive, there was a pleasing element of international co-operation. We all wanted the new tournament to be a success, so Harry Swan had no qualms about letting Djurgårdens train under the Easter Road floodlights when they arrived in Scotland – the fact this allowed Hugh Shaw to run the rule over them at close quarters was an added bonus.

Even though we would effectively have home advantage in both legs, we knew Djurgårdens would be no pushovers. Under Frank Soo, the first non-white footballer to play for England, they had won the Swedish league – or Allssvenskan – with an impressive haul of 53 goals in 22 games. The man we feared most was John Eriksson. A prolific goalscorer for his club as well as for the Swedish national team, his 17-minute hat-trick away to Gwardia Warsaw had booked Djurgårdens's place in the quarter-finals. Their captain Sigge Parling, meanwhile, had just played for Sweden in a 6-2 win over Portugal in Lisbon. He would later be part of the team to reach the 1958 World Cup Final, where a teenage Pelé would break the hosts' hearts.

Djurgårdens were, in the words of Hugh Shaw, 'a well-built, artistic lot' but what made our task even tougher was the fact that, for the second European game in succession, we would be without our star centre-forward. This time it was a heavy cold that kept Lawrie Reilly at home and Jimmy Mulkerrin was again physically handed the Hibs number nine shirt and metaphorically asked to fill one of the biggest pairs of boots in Scottish football. The near-30,000 crowd at Firhill was double that which had come to see Partick take on Spurs in a floodlight friendly just ten days earlier, but while there was plenty of noise and a fevered atmosphere, there was very little to compare the match with a Champions League quarter-final of today. There was no stirring anthem, no live television coverage, no multimillion-pound sponsorships from credit card, beer, betting or soft drinks companies. It was just 11 Scots, 11 Swedes, 44 black boots and a heavy brown football.

And while our own floodlights at Easter Road weren't perfect at that stage, they were considerably better than the ones at Firhill, which often made it difficult to judge the flight of the ball. We couldn't have got off to a worse start. Within a minute, Parling played a superb, 30-yard through ball to Birger Ekland, another Swedish international, who put Djurgårdens a goal up from 18 yards. They almost made it two after quarter of an hour when Tommy Younger was helpless as Bernt Andersson hammered the ball against the crossbar.

We took almost immediate advantage of this let-off when Gordon Smith played in Bobby Combe to fire in the equaliser from just outside the area a few minutes later. Now 31, Bobby was a fine player and a great servant who had been with the club since he was 17. A born-and-bred Leither, he'd had to spend much of his time at Easter Road in the shadow of the Famous Five, but he'd still managed to pick up three league championship medals and three Scotland caps during his career. Now the Edinburgh greengrocer had a goal in the European Cup to add to his collection.

Just after half-time, young Jimmy Mulkerrin – who was always full of running – chased down a weak back-pass and beat goalkeeper Arne Arvidsson to the ball to poke us into the lead. His strike was greeted with – it's fair to say – probably the loudest cheer for a Hibs goal ever heard at the home of Partick Thistle. We had the chance to extend our advantage when Jimmy was sandwiched between two defenders in the area but Eddie blazed the penalty wide. It was an end-to-end game and, as time was running out, we hoped to be able to grab another goal and give ourselves a cushion to take back to Edinburgh. It finally arrived in fortuitous circumstances four minutes from the end, when Eddie's shot was deflected into the net by Åke Olsson.

It had been a cracking contest and the supporters showed their appreciation to both sets of players, with Djurgårdens taking a bow in the centre circle at full-time. With no advantage for the number of 'away' goals scored in the event of an overall draw, the tie was still very much alive. And we wouldn't have to wait long before meeting them again with the second leg set to take place in Edinburgh just five days later. This was enough time for us to squeeze in another league victory, expressing our thanks to Partick for their hospitality by beating them 5-1 in Leith. Jimmy Mulkerrin was again on the scoresheet and he was then asked to deputise for Lawrie for the third European match in a row.

If the first leg against Djurgårdens in Glasgow had been a great advert for the new European Cup, the same probably couldn't be said for the second. In front of another crowd of over 30,000, one of the best opportunities in a tight match fell to Hans Andersson-Tvilling midway through the second half. But the inside-right – a football international as well as an Olympic ice hockey player – somehow fired his shot over the bar from three yards out. Jimmy Thomson played well and Bobby Combe was our biggest threat but, with the Swedes facing the exit, it was clear that this match wasn't quite the love-in that we'd experienced in Glasgow.

Referee Arthur Ellis, who had also taken charge of our previous two European ties, was no stranger to high-profile – and bad-tempered – quarter-finals. At the 1954 World Cup, the Englishman sent off three players in the notorious 'Battle of Berne' last-eight tie between Brazil and eventual finalists Hungary. He didn't send anyone for an early bath in our match, but he might have been tempted. At one point Tommy Preston went in for a tackle on Bernt Andersson. Things got rather heated between the pair, but Ellis felt it could be settled with a handshake – something that usually did the trick in those days. Andersson, however, was having none of it and refused Tommy's outstretched hand.

Djurgårdens continued to put us under pressure, especially when Willie MacFarlane had to go off for ten minutes after colliding with the barrier at the edge of the pitch. Even Willie Ormond found himself helping out in defence but Mr Ellis effectively settled the tie on 70 minutes when he awarded us a penalty after Parling hauled down Ormond in the area. The Swedes protested, but the referee was unlikely to be over-ruled on any decision by at least one of his linesmen – his younger brother, Frank. This time Eddie made no mistake and, after a string of good saves from Tommy Younger late on, we sealed our place in the semi-finals with a 4-1 aggregate win. There were, thankfully, handshakes all round at the final whistle. We all recognised that the tie was a lot closer than the scoreline suggested. Exhausted and not to mention a little bruised, we really felt we'd earned our place in the last four.

Ours had actually been the lowest-scoring and probably the least eventful of the ties. Unlike today, the matches weren't played in the same week. While we knew on 28 November 1955 that we were the first team to reach the semi-finals, fans of the new European Cup would have to wait until 12 February 1956 before learning who the fourth would be. The next couple of months did, however, see some truly remarkable scorelines across the continent.

After a 4-2 win in the first leg in Paris, French champions Stade Reims secured their place with a 4-4 draw away to MTK Budapest. Meanwhile, in front of a bumper Christmas Day crowd of 105,000 at the Bernabéu – the biggest of the competition to date – Real Madrid must have thought they were home and dry against Partizan Belgrade when they hit four without reply. The fans were grateful to their captain, Alfredo di Stéfano, for the insurance of the fourth goal when they were left clinging on in Yugoslavia, just squeaking into the semi-finals after a 3-0 defeat. Finally, Rapid Vienna had given themselves a fighting chance against mighty AC Milan after a 1-1 draw in Austria, only for the Italians to run riot at the San Siro with a 7-2 victory.

When all matches were finally completed, the full semi-final line-up would see Real Madrid versus AC Milan and Stade Reims take on Hibs. In other words, the national champions of Italy, the national champions of Spain and the national champions of France joined by the team which had finished fifth in Scotland. On viewing the draw, we were clearly the odd ones out, but anyone who had watched the way we'd played against the finest teams from Sweden and West Germany could see that we weren't just there to make up the numbers.

And our lofty position among Europe's elite would soon be reflected in the league. After a late winner from Jimmy Mulkerrin gave us a victory at St Mirren, our 6-3 win at home to Dundee on 10 December saw us replace Celtic at the top of the table with a game in hand. Our early setback in the League Cup didn't seem to matter. Lawrie had returned and we still had three trophies to play for. We were on a high. We only hoped it would last.

5

Broken Reims

WE'VE ALL been there. Or I like to think most of us have. Getting called into the head teacher's office is rarely a good thing, and I started to have flashbacks to my days at Bellshill Academy when I was summoned to see Hugh Shaw after our dismal Scottish Cup defeat to Raith Rovers. I got the message to go and see him during training and had difficulty concentrating for the rest of the session. After the way we'd played during our 3-1 defeat in Kirkcaldy, I can't say I was expecting the boss to offer me a raise in my salary, but it felt like a punch to the gut when he said he was going to 'rest' me for the next match. I might only have been 18, but even I knew that 'rest' was simply code for 'drop'.

At the time I tried to put a brave face on it, going so far as to tell a newspaper afterwards that I was actually 'relieved' about being left on the sidelines because I knew that I'd been playing badly. I don't believe those words any more now than I did when I said them. Of course I wasn't relieved – I was gutted, as any player would be. I did my best to hide my disappointment, thanked the manager and headed off for one of the longest days of work I'd ever had.

Believing that you've been singled out or in any way blamed for a side's collective failure isn't easy, especially when you're only young. The feeling that comes with being dropped makes everything in a footballer's life so much harder. Getting out of bed becomes more of a slog, the journey to the ground seems to take a hell of a lot longer and, worst of all, you know that the first team are off to play in front of tens of thousands of adoring fans while you're sent to play in front of a handful of spectators with the reserves. I think I found it especially hard because I'd been in the first team virtually from the day I walked through the gates at Easter Road. Playing alongside people like Gordon Smith, Lawrie Reilly, Eddie Turnbull and the rest had become second nature. I'd never really known anything different. For better or worse, being a constant in the Hibs line-up had given me a sense of entitlement, but it also gave me a determination to try harder than ever to regain my place.

Things had been looking so rosy in the lead-up to Christmas 1955. Not only had we reached the semi-finals of the European Cup, but we also topped the recently renamed Scottish League Division One. Following the restructuring of the league, this was actually a greater achievement than it had been in previous seasons. The top flight had been expanded from 16 teams to 18 with the promotion of Airdrie and Dunfermline Athletic, while Division Two had been stretched from 16 teams to 19 as five new sides joined the league.

We were playing well and, for the first time in a few seasons, the table reflected this. But just as Hibs fans were preparing to tuck into their turkey with their team top of the league, the Old Firm hit us with the old one-two to knock the collective stuffing out of us. On 17 December we lost 4-1 at Ibrox in a match so full of questionable refereeing decisions that even Lawrie Reilly received a rare booking for contesting a penalty awarded to Rangers. We had actually taken the lead on 17 minutes through Willie Ormond, but the penalty, given on 65 minutes, would see us go 3-1 down. And there was little doubt among the home support, or any of us for that matter, that Johnny Hubbard was going to put the spot-kick away. He wasn't known as the 'Penalty King' for nothing, with the South African winger eventually clocking up an enviable record at Rangers of 63 out of 66 attempts converted. He had already achieved legendary status at the club the previous season when he became the first foreign player to score a hat-trick for Rangers against Celtic, and in the competition's second season, he became the first South African to play in the European Cup. But it was for his deadly accuracy from the spot that Hubbard was most famous, and his successful penalty that day put the game beyond doubt.

We hoped to make amends when we welcomed Celtic to Easter Road on Christmas Eve but it turned out to be another match to be remembered for all the wrong reasons. With the score at 3-1 to Celtic, Eddie pulled a goal back to make it 3-2 on 80 minutes. We felt we were in the ascendancy and were getting close to drawing level when the referee, Ernest Youngson from Aberdeen, inexplicably blew the final whistle when there were nearly four minutes remaining. There were actually three minutes and 44 seconds left to play according to a man from the BBC, who shared with his colleagues in the press box a chronometer he was using for the split-second timing of his tape recording. Boos from the majority of the 32,000 fans rang around the stadium. A couple of us went up to the referee to find out what was going on, and we were relieved to see one of his linesmen running on to the pitch. Great, we thought, he'll be here to point out the mistake and we'll still have a few minutes left to try to score the equaliser. But we were dismayed to see him simply hold out his hand to congratulate the man in the middle on a job well done. It seems that, unlike spotting offsides, fouls, handballs, foul throws and rude gestures from wingers, spotting when a referee accidentally cuts a game short isn't in an assistant's remit.

For us it was a case of 'Fergie Time' in reverse. We wouldn't necessarily have scored, of course, but for those who doubt whether those extra four minutes (plus time added on for stoppages) would have made any difference, I just need to point out that Ferguson's Manchester United needed only two minutes of injury time to turn the 1999 Champions League Final on its head to secure the third and final part of their historic treble. Besides, when you've got 'Last Minute' Reilly on your side, four minutes is ample time to change a result. I joked at the time that Mr Youngson had mistakenly set his watch to the clock on the North British Hotel (now the Balmoral) on Princes Street. Since 1902, coincidentally the last year Hibs had won the Scottish Cup up to that point, the clock has famously run three minutes fast so that passengers are less likely to be late when catching the train from nearby Waverley Station. Whatever the reason for the error, Celtic weren't complaining. Their 3-2 win put them top of the league, while Harry Swan made a late addition to his Christmas list – a great big clock for the Easter Road stand.

For those of you not from Scotland, New Year's Eve – or Hogmanay as we call it – is rather a big deal, particularly in Edinburgh, which might explain why only 10,000 fans turned out for our final match of the year, at home to bottom-of-the-table Stirling Albion. While it's obvious that the Binos are never going to be as big a draw as Celtic, we were disappointed with the low turnout, although I have to admit that 31 December in Leith can be a bit on the chilly side – no matter how many Hogmanay drams you've had. The hardy Hibees who had come to watch the football were in for a treat, however, as braces from Bobby Combe and Gordon Smith, and one goal each from Lawrie and Willie Ormond, saw us beat Stirling 6-1. It was the second time in the space of three weeks that we'd hit six goals although, had Mr Youngson been in charge, we might only have won 5-1, with Gordon's second goal arriving in the 87th minute. We were still in fourth place, but things were tight at the top. We were level on points with Hearts and Rangers, while Celtic, who had played two games more than their Old Firm rivals, were three points clear.

We began 1956 with a thrilling derby against Hearts at Easter Road, which was very much a case of easy-come, easy-go. All four goals in the 2-2 draw were scored within eight dizzying minutes in the second half. Lawrie and Willie sent our fans into raptures by putting us two up but, before you could say 'Edinburgh bragging rights', Willie Bauld and Alfie Conn had levelled things. Bobby Combe, who had been scoring plenty of goals all season, was left kicking himself after blazing a late opportunity over the bar from close range. And when I say close range, I mean Bobby really couldn't have been any closer. He was almost in the goal when the ball came to him. Anyone watching would have put their house on Bobby scoring because it would have been impossible to kick the ball over the bar from there, but somehow he managed it. If it had been at the other end, then I'd have been patting him on the back for a world-class clearance. But these things happen, even to the best of footballers.

We set aside this massive disappointment with wins over Clyde and Kilmarnock, but Aberdeen continued to be our bogey side by recording their seventh victory over us in a row. Things started to look up again when we beat Motherwell at home in spectacular fashion. All five members of our forward line – including Bobby – were on the scoresheet in a 7-0 win. Eddie netted a hat-trick in what was our best result of the season and it completed a miserable double for Motherwell fans, who had watched Hearts hammer their team 7-1 at Tynecastle the previous month. They would probably have to be dragged kicking and screaming on to the supporters' bus the next time it was setting off for Edinburgh.

But our own performances, particularly with the number of goals we were scoring, meant we weren't particularly concerned to have been drawn against Raith Rovers in round five of the Scottish Cup, the point where Division One teams entered the fray. We'd already beaten them 4-0 in Fife earlier in the season and they sat below Motherwell in the table. We weren't expecting to score another seven goals, but the fact we'd been handed the home draw meant we felt pretty good about our chances of making it through to the next round for the first time in three seasons. But while they'd failed to take a league point from us in

Edinburgh at the last six times of asking, Raith also had a knack of making life difficult for us in the cup, most recently three years earlier when they beat us 4-1 after two replays. Our odds looked to have improved when the original Saturday fixture was postponed and, to our surprise, Raith agreed to play the tie under floodlights the following Wednesday night.

Evening kick-offs, after all, seemed to suit us; you only needed to ask fans of Rot-Weiss Essen, Djurgårdens, Preston North End, Newcastle United, Manchester City and Manchester United, all of whom we'd beaten under the lights in recent months. And while an evening friendly we were due to play against Tottenham Hotspur on the Monday couldn't now go ahead, the rearranged fixture meant that Hibs were about to make yet another piece of history. Alongside the match between East Fife and Stenhousemuir at Bayview, which had also been postponed, Hibs versus Raith Rovers on 8 February 1956 was the first Scottish Cup tie to be played under floodlights. Incidentally, Hibs actually played Stenhousemuir in Scotland's very first floodlit match, in November 1951, beating them 5-3 at Ochilview. But this was very much an experiment and, in all honesty, the players – let alone the fans – would have done well to see the ball. You'd probably get more wattage from the bulb in your car's glove compartment than from those early makeshift floodlights. Nevertheless, it showed that football could be played under artificial light and paved the way for our Scottish Cup tie against Raith.

Had any of us read the Hibs programme we'd have seen a warning of what was to come in – albeit now somewhat dated – black and white. 'Cup-tie football differs greatly from the ordinary trend of league games,' it read, 'for clubs stationed near the foot of the ladder can summon new energy and determination in an effort to raise the morale of themselves and the club. Therefore every club must be treated as equal, and you can bet your bottom dollar the men from Stark's Park care not the slightest for the result of the last match [our 4-0 win in Kirkcaldy].'

Wise words which we'd all have done well to heed. That 'new energy and determination' from the opposition nearly saw us knocked out of the cup in front of our own fans and we were very lucky to take the tie to a replay when Eddie, following up Lawrie's saved shot, fired in an equaliser with only a couple of minutes left. The replay would take place at Stark's Park on 13 February, which gave us enough time before then to lose in the league to Falkirk. This, again, was a big disappointment, as a win at Brockville would have put us level on points with Hearts in second place. The inconsistency of our form was incredibly frustrating for us as players, so I can only imagine what it must have been like to be watching us from the stands.

Although I'd played pretty well in the first match against Raith, I'm the first to admit that I wasn't at my best at Stark's Park and Ernie Copland, a great goalscorer and a member of Scotland's 1954 World Cup squad, took full advantage. Ernie had a terrific game and scored twice in a 3-1 win, ensuring Hibs' 54-year wait to lift the Scottish Cup would continue for at least another season. While we were, of course, all blissfully unaware that the club's long wait to get their hands on the famous trophy would carry on into the next millennium, we were all hugely disappointed to go out at the first time of asking for the second season running.

We were slated for the defeat but, in retrospect, perhaps we shouldn't have felt too badly about succumbing to Rovers. Bert Herdman's side reached the semi-finals that season and it took eventual winners Hearts – who had so easily swept us aside in the previous year's competition – two attempts to knock them out. I can't explain why I didn't play well. All I can say is that footballers aren't robots. Unfortunately, with the semi-finals of the European Cup on the horizon, my timing was far from ideal. To put things in perspective, the night before we lost to Raith, Milan were booking their place in the semi-finals with a 7-2 win over Rapid Vienna at the San Siro. If we were to upset the odds and find a way past Stade Reims, the formidable Italians looked likely to be our opponents in the final, but that really would have been getting ahead of ourselves.

Next up in the league were newly promoted Dunfermline Athletic, against whom Hugh Shaw decided to hand a competitive debut – along with my number five shirt – to 19-year-old Bobby Nicol. Although I was a team player and supportive of a fellow teenager, I have to confess that a small, selfish part of me hoped that young Bobby's first outing in a Hibs jersey wouldn't be a complete success. Fat chance. Another hat-trick from Eddie helped ensure Bobby enjoyed a dream debut – they won 7-1 in front of 18,000 fans, but it might at least give our French opponents something to worry about.

Unsurprisingly, Bobby retained his place in the next match against Airdrie, but a 3-1 defeat saw me back in the side for the following game against, would you believe it, Raith Rovers. We were now only three weeks away from our semi-final and I was desperate to participate in Paris, where it had been agreed that Reims would play their home tie at the Parc des Princes. The French champions had some excellent players, including the magnificent centre-half Robert Jonquet, who had been a mainstay for the national side – *Les Bleus* – for the last eight years and would reach greater heights in 1958, captaining France to a third-place finish at the World Cup. Up front, Léon Glovacki and Réne Bliard were both in contention to be the European Cup's first top scorer having already found the net nine times between them. And in Michel Hidalgo, Reims had a man who, as national team manager nearly 30 years later, would lead France to their first major trophy – the 1984 European Championships.

But no player in the Reims line-up commanded more respect than Raymond Kopa, the gifted playmaker whose performances in Europe would help earn him a dream move to Real Madrid the following season. In a team of stars at the Santiago Bernabéu he was the one who eventually shone brightest, winning the Ballon d'Or as the best player in Europe in 1958. But if I was going to line up against Stade Reims, I would first have to play well against Raith Rovers. And if I was going to take on Raymond Kopa, I'd first need to try to contain Ernie Copland. Despite going well in the cup, recent defeats in the league had seen Raith being dragged down towards the relegation zone. It was true that they had failed to take a solitary point away from Easter Road during six and a half seasons in the top flight, but they were getting desperate.

Andy King gave them a first-half lead, but we went ahead through goals from Willie Ormond and then Gordon Smith. But just when it was starting to look like we might enjoy a modicum of revenge for our cup defeat, Bernie Kelly – a young lad from my neck of the woods in Holytown – equalised less than a quarter of an hour from the end. I look back on this 2-2 draw now as significant as it turned out to be my last first-team involvement of the season. I still held out hope that I would be in the manager's plans for our big date in Paris, but my prospects now appeared bleaker than ever.

John Grant, normally a half-back, played centre-half in the next three league games, during which Hibs earned two wins and a draw. I couldn't deny John the opportunity and I'm definitely not sure I could ever have shown his level of patience. In stark contrast to my own route into the first team, John had had to wait five long years after signing – from 1949 to 1954 – before making his league debut for Hibs at the age of 23. And there was now someone else standing in my way. The first of the three league matches, against East Fife, saw the long-awaited return of Archie Buchanan. A fellow joiner, he was one of the unsung heroes of Hibs' three championship-winning campaigns of 1948, 1951 and 1952. He'd suffered a bad leg break against Aberdeen in September 1954, an event which had undoubtedly played a part in me being handed my debut so quickly. It had been a long road to recovery for Archie and, during his recuperation, I remember watching him running up and down, up and down the terracing at Easter Road, trying to rebuild the strength in his leg. He had been back playing reserve-team football since January and the timing of his return to full fitness had been impeccable. While his team-mates and fans were delighted to see Archie return, although perhaps not to his previous best, the fact Hugh felt that we needed his experience at centre-half ultimately cost me any chance of playing in Paris.

As I've said, I wasn't worldly, but even I'd heard of the Eiffel Tower, the Louvre and the Champs-Élysées and I'd hoped to be able to enjoy them in some capacity while in the French capital. While I did fly with my team-mates in the end, it was merely as a passenger. The fact I wasn't on the team sheet against Reims was enough to take some of the shine off the attractions, but I did enjoy our stay in the Grand Hotel Terminus (now Hilton Paris Opera). It wasn't the kind of place I could ever have imagined staying in while growing up in a Lanarkshire tenement. The hotel was just a 45-minute walk to the Eiffel Tower and while several of the more senior players – including our well-known Francophile captain Gordon Smith – had been to Paris before, some of the other young players and I could barely wait to explore. We were up on the monument within a couple of hours of our arrival.

Much like today, the tower was crawling with camera-wielding tourists, so we found it hard to believe that, when we were little boys, Adolf Hitler had stood on this spot, admiring the magnificent city his Nazi forces had conquered. Indeed, it had been just ten years since the Eiffel Tower's lift cables, which were cut ahead of the invasion to ensure the Nazis had to climb the stairs, had been repaired. That was good news for us. We may have been young, fit professional footballers but it's still a hell of a climb to the top, which was undergoing repairs following a fire a few months earlier. Gazing out as the sun slowly sank over that amazing Parisian skyline gave me a sense of perspective. I'm only 18, I told myself. I've got my whole career – my whole life – ahead of me. Yes, I was disappointed not to be playing the following evening in what would have been my biggest match so far, but there would be other opportunities down the line. Who knew? If things went really well, we could all be returning to France in a couple of months' time for the final. Stranger things had happened.

I was proud to have played my part in getting us to this stage in this new competition, particularly in that opening 4-0 win over Rot-Weiss Essen. I was also proud of the way we'd performed as a team. No matter what happened next, we had done Scotland credit and silenced those who felt that the side which had finished fifth the previous season would stand absolutely no chance against Europe's elite. Besides, I wasn't the only one to be disappointed at missing out in Paris. Tommy Preston hadn't been selected either, meaning that Tiger Thomson was the only member of Scotland's youngest half-back line to play against Reims. All Tommy and I could do now was wish our friends good luck and take our seats alongside the rest of the fans at the Parc des Princes.

As I had expected, it turned out to be a reasonably even game in front of a partisan crowd of more than 35,000. Kopa, who was nicknamed 'The Little General', was on great form, but Archie also played well, as did John Grant. Reims didn't manage to score until midway through the second half through Michel Leblond. We had our chances, but Bliard popped up with a killer second goal with under a minute to go. Our hearts sank. It was our first defeat in the competition and the first time that we'd failed to score. We were all a bit deflated, especially with the second goal arriving so late, but there was one thing guaranteed to perk up a group of young footballers – and that was a trip to the Moulin Rouge. Somehow the sight of those can-can girls in full flow took the sting out of the defeat, at least for a few hours.

Reims must have been glad of the insurance of Bliard's goal when they flew into Edinburgh a fortnight later. Despite us, in the words of Eddie, 'battering them silly' in front of 45,000 fans at Easter Road, Kopa set up Glovacki with a superb pass in the second half to put the tie beyond our reach. After seven months we'd reached the end of the line. There was no doubt among the pundits or the players that Kopa was the man who made the difference. I felt the 3-0 aggregate defeat wasn't an accurate reflection of how we'd performed, but maybe that's just me looking at the tie through green-tinted spectacles. It's always tempting in these situations – so near and yet so far – to consider what might have been. To this day, whether I'm in the middle of a round of golf or if I'm taking the dog for a walk, I occasionally find myself thinking about that match and wondering: what if I had played at centre-half in the semi-final? Would I have been able to tame Kopa? As Lawrie – who knew a fair bit about getting the better of defenders – pointed out, I was a footballing centre-half and not just a stopper. But I'll never know and, as Kopa himself might say, *c'est la vie*.

The following evening in Spain, Real Madrid took a giant step towards joining our French conquerors in the final with a 4-2 first-leg victory over AC Milan. Two Giorgio Dal Monte penalties saw the Rossoneri win the second leg 2-1 at the San Siro, but José Villalonga's men booked their ticket to Paris with a 4-3 victory on aggregate.

The final itself was a fitting end to a memorable tournament and marked the start of a five-year period of dominance by the Spaniards. Reims made a blistering start with Leblond and Jean Templin putting them two goals up inside ten minutes, but not even the magic of Kopa could stop Real from securing the first of five consecutive titles with a 4-3 victory. Not that it would have caused him too much concern. Having caught his opponents' eye with his performances in the inaugural competition, he was soon on his way to the Bernabéu where he helped Real to their next three European Cup wins, including beating Reims 2-0 in the 1959 final.

For Real Madrid and for football fans around the world, the adventure was just beginning. For Hibs and for me, it was all over. If we ever wanted to compete again in what would quickly become an illustrious competition, a fifth-place finish in our domestic league would certainly never be good enough. Hibs still had four league matches to play, but my season had already finished. Rangers won the league with three matches to spare, beating defending champions Aberdeen under the Ibrox floodlights to secure their 29th title. Of our last four matches, the high point was a 3-0 win at Parkhead although, by that stage, Celtic could only finish fifth. We went one better than the previous season, finishing level on points with third-placed Hearts and only a point behind Aberdeen.

A lot of the talk in the newspapers after I'd been dropped focused on whether or not I was 'burnt out'. At the time I laughed it off. I was still a teenager. When we beat St Mirren after clinching our place in the European Cup semi-final, I was asked by a reporter whether an 18-year-old can play too much.

'Definitely not,' I replied, which shows how much I knew. Up to the point I was left out of the side, I'd played in 34 competitive matches in succession since the start of the season, plus all five of our Floodlit Challenge matches. The only other ever-present in the side up to that point was Eddie Turnbull, but he wasn't commuting from Lanarkshire, working as a joiner and leading a Boys' Brigade PE class once a week. It wasn't a case of me burning the candle at both ends but setting fire to it in the middle as well. Like most teenagers – particularly those who play sport – I felt invincible, but I don't think there's any doubt that fatigue had begun to have an effect on my performances towards the end of the season.

I think clubs today try to take a bit more care of their young players and use them sparingly when possible but, even as recently as Michael Owen, it wasn't always the case. The former Liverpool, Real Madrid and England striker attributed his long list of injury worries to being overplayed as a youngster, accelerating his fall from Ballon d'Or winner to warming the bench at Stoke City. And a future team-mate of mine, Joe Baker, who was also a regular in the Hibs side from the age of 17, was scoring a fraction of the goals he used to score by the time he was just 27. Of course there are exceptions – Pelé being the ultimate example. But these were different times, and I like to think football has learned a thing or two since my day.

As for our history-making campaign on the continent, some younger football fans might think it's a bit of an anomaly to see Hibs listed as European Cup semi-finalists. But like any competition, it takes time to bed in. Don't forget that the very first World Cup, held in Uruguay in 1930, saw the USA finish third – a heady height the Americans have never reached since. I doubt we'll ever see Hibs reach that stage of the competition again. Indeed, they've never played in it since, but there's no doubt that with our opening game in particular, when we swept aside the German champions on their own doorstep, we played our part in making the inaugural competition a success.

Gordon Smith, who remarkably would play in the semi-final of the European Cup for Dundee seven years later, said, 'There was an insular, even ignorant attitude in Scotland as well as in England. There was still a belief that it was *our* game, and that the continentals should not be taken too seriously.'

Real Madrid, in particular, had changed all that, and I wasn't giving up the thought of one day playing against them.

6

Curses

I COULDN'T help myself. It was pure instinct. From somewhere deep inside there came a guttural roar that only football fans can truly understand. 'YEEEES!' I shouted and leapt to my feet, punching the air in triumph and doing the closest thing to a Highland jig you'll catch me doing these days. The dog was going mad, my wife Susan ran through from the kitchen to find out what the commotion was and my mug of tea had somehow ended up halfway across the living room. But broken crockery and a stained carpet didn't stop me wanting to crack open the champagne. In the 93rd minute of one of the most pulsating matches I'd seen in years, David Gray, the Hibernian captain, had just ended one of the most famous curses in sport.

The date was 21 May 2016 and, with a 3-2 win over Rangers at Hampden Park, my former club had won the Scottish Cup for the first time since 1902 – 114 years of hurt were finally over. Fans of the Boston Red Sox – with their 'Curse of the Bambino' – don't know they're born. After star player Babe Ruth was sold to arch-rivals the New York Yankees in 1918, Red Sox fans had to wait a mere 86 years before regaining baseball's World Series. At the time of the Babe's $125,000 transfer, Hibs' Scottish Cup curse had already been in full swing for 16 years, and it would go on for another decade after Red Sox fans were finally able to celebrate. Legend has it that the Hibs curse began in the 1950s when an Irish woman of gypsy heritage was angry about the club's harp emblem – a symbol of its Irish heritage – not being returned to the south stand following a period of refurbishment at Easter Road. It's an interesting tale, but it doesn't explain the first half-century of failure to recapture the trophy, including appearances in the finals of 1914, 1923, 1924 and 1947.

Maybe it was a curse, maybe Harry Swan had walked under too many ladders or maybe it was a simple case of Hibs being outplayed on the big day seven times in a row. Whatever the reason for the lack of success, the main point was that the 2016 Scottish Cup victory had been a long, long time in coming. Between Bobby Atherton and David Gray being handed the trophy, the world had seen – among one or two other things – the invention of the aeroplane, the sinking of the *Titanic*, two world wars and men walking on the Moon. Empires had crumbled, 27 Prime Ministers had lived in 10 Downing Street and The Beatles had said 'Hello, Goodbye', but there was one constant. Hibs still hadn't won the Scottish Cup. Many wonderful players who have graced the turf at Easter Road – including every member of the Famous Five, plus Joe Baker, Pat Stanton and Peter Cormack – never got to experience the joy that Gray and his team-mates were experiencing at that moment. Indeed, Lawrie Reilly said that not winning the Scottish Cup was the biggest regret of his career. That regret as a player turned into an even greater regret as a fan – he didn't live long enough to see his team win the trophy.

That's to say nothing of all the other supporters who were born and had died without ever seeing the Hibs colours tied to the famous piece of silverware. I didn't want to tempt fate beforehand by making a prediction – even to myself – but I did have a good feeling this time, probably because Hibs had managed to knock out Raith Rovers and Hearts on their way to the final. But what turned out to be a fairytale ending had so nearly been the old, familiar story. Anthony Stokes – on loan from Celtic – had put Hibs ahead after only three minutes, only for Kenny Miller to equalise. Then, midway through the second half, Andy Halliday put Rangers ahead. It was the kind of sublime strike that makes you realise it might not be your day.

Maybe it was because Stokes was on loan that he didn't feel the weight of history bearing down on him. Having already gone close several times, he equalised on 80 minutes and then, just when we looked like we'd be going into the 30 minutes of torture known as extra time, Gray powered home a header from Liam Henderson's corner. Grown men wept, cats and dogs embraced, and the curse – at long last – was lifted. The drought might not have been so intolerable had it not been for the fact that, on the other side of Edinburgh, Hearts fans had watched their team win the Scottish Cup three times in the space of 14 years. Their most recent win came in a match that, to Hibs supporters, is like Lord Voldemort to Harry Potter and his pals – it's the final that must not be named.

As far as they're concerned, the only football results of note on 19 May 2012 were Chelsea beating Bayern Munich in the

Champions League Final, West Ham United getting the better of Blackpool in the Championship play-off final and Jamaica defeating Guyana 1-0 in a friendly. That's because the first meeting between Hibs and Hearts in a Scottish Cup Final since 1896 didn't go quite as well as those in the east of Edinburgh had hoped. The Famous Five had been replaced by the Infamous 5-1 – the most one-sided final in 16 years – when Hearts lost to Rangers by the same scoreline, and even harder to take than Hibs' 6-1 loss to Celtic in 1972. The match was preceded by a campaign by the *Edinburgh Evening News* to relocate the final to the city and Murrayfield, the home of Scottish rugby. I couldn't understand that. Quite apart from the logistics of changing the venue at the last minute, fans look forward to their day out to the national football stadium – it's a huge part of the magic of the cup. Besides, it's less than 50 miles between the two cities. Pity those English fans who had to fly 2,000 miles to Moscow to watch Manchester United take on Chelsea in the 2008 Champion League Final.

It's probably a toss-up for Hibs fans about what was worse on the day of the 5-1 – the heavy defeat to their local rivals or the fact that, once again, they had failed to take their chance on the big stage. I know how much the cup final means to Hibs supporters and I know how disappointing it is to lose, because I had been there, done that, and picked up the runners-up medal.

The 1958 showpiece against Clyde was the first time Hibs had reached the Scottish Cup Final since 1947. That had been the first staging of the competition since before the Second World War and, despite a first-minute goal from Jock Cuthbertson, they lost 2-1 to Aberdeen, with the trophy heading to the north-east of Scotland for the first time. After being dropped towards the end of the 1955/56 season in the wake of our early cup exit to Raith Rovers, I was approaching the start of the new campaign in a different frame of mind. Before, I'd been sure of my place in the starting line-up. Now nothing was guaranteed, but I was determined not to let it get me down. As I'd said to myself while I was up the Eiffel Tower, I was still only 18 and my whole career lay ahead of me. I was reminded of that moment when I visited the English equivalent during a week-long family holiday to Blackpool. It wasn't all ice cream and donkey rides, however, and I spent many hours running up and down the Golden Mile to help get myself fit for the new season.

There had been a few changes over the summer, most notably the £9,000 transfer of our goalkeeper Tommy Younger to Liverpool. Tommy was now Scotland's regular number one, so 20-year-old reserve Jackie Wren knew he had a big pair of gloves to fill when he made his Hibs debut on the opening day of the season – away to Hearts in the League Cup. I wasn't selected, which, from a personal point of view, was probably just as well. We were thrashed 6-1 by the Scottish Cup holders in a match which my unfortunate namesake also had to face – and was subsequently beaten by – two penalties from Bobby Kirk. Also making his debut was wing-half Davie Laing, who had spent the first eight years of his career at Tynecastle before winning the Scottish Cup with Clyde in 1955.

Jackie managed to save a spot-kick from Falkirk's Eddie O'Hara in the next match but couldn't stop Hibs from losing 1-0. Another new signing, Hugh Higgins – a wing-half who had also attracted interest from Celtic and Sunderland – made his debut and it was clear the side was struggling to gel. The Falkirk defeat was followed by a 4-0 loss to eventual finalists Partick Thistle, which meant that, once again, we had fallen at the first hurdle in the League Cup. I was finally given the nod at centre-half over John Grant for the fourth match, the return visit of Hearts. The horror show of the season opener didn't stop 40,000 fans showing up to Easter Road and the performance was considerably better, despite the fact we lost 2-1. We were beaten 4-0 away by Falkirk in the next match, which by this point was meaningless, but we soon got our revenge at Easter Road in the first league game of the season as Lawrie Reilly scored a hat-trick in a 6-1 victory. I was joined in the half-back line by Hugh Higgins and the ever-versatile Bobby Combe.

Opening the scoring that day was 20-year-old John Fraser, a nice lad from Portobello who made his Hibs debut just a few weeks after my own. Strong competition meant that he was limited to just 11 appearances in his first two seasons, but it was in this campaign that he really started to establish himself and he would eventually make nearly 300 appearances for the club. It was our best opening-day result since the championship-winning campaign of 1950/51, but it's a good job we didn't let the result go to our heads. Three straight defeats followed, to Queen of the South, Hearts (again) and then – make sure you're sitting down – Aberdeen. The 3-1 loss at Pittodrie was notable only because it marked the first appearance of another goalkeeper, Lawrie Leslie. Although signed from Junior side Newtongrange Star at the beginning of the season, Lawrie wasn't always able to get away from his National Service duty down in Shropshire.

Despite the result, Lawrie showed enough to make us think that he might be the one to assume Tommy Younger's mantle as Hibs' number one. He kept five clean sheets in the 12 matches he played that season and would go on to become a Scotland international as well as a firm favourite at Airdrie, West Ham United, Stoke City and Millwall.

I was out of the side again after the Aberdeen game and I had to watch with the horrified supporters as we went a further seven matches without a win. By the time we lost 3-0 to fellow strugglers Partick Thistle in mid-November – Archie Buchanan's last game for the club – we were sitting fourth from bottom in the table and only two points above the relegation zone. It was Hibs' worst start to a league season for more than quarter of a century. The signs weren't great especially as that season, 1930/31, they'd lost to Leith Athletic and were then relegated. Despite still having Lawrie Reilly, Eddie Turnbull, Gordon Smith and Willie Ormond at the club, the glory days of the Famous Five were now a memory fading faster than anyone cared to acknowledge. Spurs and Newcastle helped see to it that even our Floodlit Challenge matches, where we'd so often felt invincible, were now being lost.

From a personal point of view, I at least had the small consolation that my commute had become a lot easier. I'd moved out of the family home in Holytown to a flat on Leith Walk. It was hardly palatial but it was a short walk to Easter Road and, almost as importantly, it was close to the now-demolished Alhambra Cinema. Like today, 'The Walk' was a very lively, bustling place which was ever-evolving. This was a significant year because it saw the very last of the original Edinburgh trams trundle to a halt at the Shrub Hill depot. The mode of transport had been scrapped because they were considered 'inflexible' compared to the city's buses. At the time of writing, millions of pounds is being spent digging up large swathes of Leith Walk as part of Edinburgh's new tram project. Sometimes it's funny how things work out.

I made the move to Edinburgh despite now having something – or rather, someone – back in Lanarkshire to take my mind off my lack of playing time. I had first met Anne Hunter at primary school, but we then went our separate ways. While she attended the famous Dalziel High School in Motherwell, where she was head girl and went on to train as a radiographer, I went to Bellshill Academy. We stayed in touch and had been 'going steady', as they said in those days, for several months. But we both agreed that it would make my life a lot easier if I could walk to work.

I managed to get myself back in the team to face St Mirren in mid-December and we were grateful to Eddie Turnbull for rescuing a draw with only five minutes to go. It also saw yet another new face, this time that of Pat Hughes, appearing alongside me at half-back. This marked the start of a seven-match unbeaten run with some truly excellent results, including a 2-0 win over league leaders Hearts and a 4-1 victory over Aberdeen. Two goals from Lawrie Reilly and one each from Willie Ormond and John Fraser had helped us to our first league win over the Dons in nearly three years. It was now January 1957 and we had fought tooth and claw – which included having to play four games in only eight days – to get to a comparatively magnificent seventh place in the table. But we were still a long way off the pace and it was clear that the Scottish Cup was our best chance of silverware. Despite going out in the first round on the last two occasions, we had at least some cause for optimism because we'd been handed a home tie against Aberdeen, the team we'd just beaten so convincingly. I say 'some' cause for optimism because, a week before the cup tie, Raith Rovers – who knocked us out the previous year – thumped us in the league. As before, our inconsistency was our undoing.

And 2 February 1957, the day of the match – or should I say matches – got off to an ominous start. With little sense of planning, and even less common sense, Edinburgh came close to breaking point as we hosted Aberdeen, Hearts played Rangers at Tynecastle and, over at Murrayfield, Scotland took on Wales in what was then the Five Nations Championship. The fixtures saw a combined attendance of around 130,000 fans and, unsurprisingly, all leave was cancelled for the city's police officers. Before any of the games kicked off, a train full of rugby supporters travelling up from the Borders crashed into the buffers at Waverley Station and six people were taken to hospital. Thankfully, none of them were seriously hurt.

In the home dressing room at Easter Road we were oblivious to the chaos. It was another Scottish Cup campaign and, after a poor season in the league, we felt we owed our supporters a decent run. As it transpired, we would have to give them a collective IOU. As I mentioned earlier, I've never been someone to leave a football match early. As far as I'm concerned, win, lose or draw, you should be there with your team when that final whistle blows. Having said that, if any of those loyal Hibbies had decided they wanted to get out of Easter Road and drown their sorrows with an early pint at half-time, I don't think I could have blamed them. We conceded a goal to Graham Leggat after only three minutes, before Bobby Wishart (two) and Harry Yorston combined to put us 4-0 down with barely half an hour on the clock. And although we rallied – or Reilleyed – in the second half with goals from Lawrie, Gordon Smith and Bobby Nicol, the 4-3 defeat proved to be another bitter Scottish Cup pill to swallow. The only slight consolation for our supporters was that, across the capital, an equally rampant Rangers had put four without reply past Hearts.

We frequently hear today's managers complain about fixture congestion, but the phrase didn't seem to exist back in the 1950s. The whistle had barely left the referee's lips before Harry Swan was on the phone to Leicester City, inviting them to play a friendly at Easter Road because we now had a gap in our schedule. Leicester were now being managed by former Aberdeen boss Dave Halliday and, to rub an extra dose of salt into our cup wounds, Ian McNeill, whom he had taken with him to Filbert Street, scored twice in a 3-2 win. We could only hope that, in the following season, there would be no such gaps in our schedule to fill. But if we were to have any chance of finally breaking the curse, we'd need the help of a very special player – and we were lucky that there was one waiting in the wings.

Before then, I came up against one of the all-time greats during that summer's Edinburgh Select charity match. A regular fixture in the city's football calendar from 1944 to 1962, the annual event saw Hibs and Hearts players combine to take on one of the top English sides at either Easter Road or Tynecastle. This time, we had the pleasure of welcoming Preston North

End and England legend Tom Finney to Leith. When I say pleasure, it wasn't so pleasurable at one point, when Finney twisted, turned and then left me on my backside before firing home a shot from 25 yards in Preston's 3-1 win. He turned to me afterwards and said, 'You're really good, Jackie. Don't worry about that. You'll be all right.' I really appreciated those words from the great man.

I'd been fortunate in my young career to be a first-hand witness to some historic Hibernian moments. Not only was I part of the first British side to play in Europe, but I was also on the pitch the last time the Famous Five played together. On 14 August 1957, I was in the starting line-up to witness another notable occasion: the debut of Joseph Henry Baker. Joe had been scoring goals by the truckload in the reserves and had a confidence that belied his years, so nobody was surprised when he made his first appearance against Airdrie in the League Cup at the age of just 17 years and 28 days. Although, I have to point out, he was positively long in the tooth compared to one Jackie Plenderleith, who made his debut at 17 years and 24 days, not to mention the man Joe replaced as the club's number nine, Lawrie Reilly, who was still a couple of weeks shy of his 17th birthday when he made his Hibs bow in 1945.

Born in Liverpool, Joe and his elder brother Gerry – who at this point was playing for Motherwell – grew up in Wishaw, just five miles from Holytown. So despite a thick Lanarkshire accent much like my own, Joe's 'accident of birth' meant he was only eligible to play for England, which he did on eight occasions between 1959 and 1966. He was even in Alf Ramsey's initial 40-man squad for the World Cup. But while Joe missed out on a chance at immortality in an England shirt, his 158 goals in 194 games during two spells at Easter Road made the 'Wishae' lad a Hibs legend. And there was one Scottish Cup match, in particular, during his first season – 1957/58 – that truly marked Joe out for greatness. First up, however, was the League Cup and, despite wins in all three of our home fixtures – against East Fife, Celtic and Airdrie – we were once again unable to progress to the quarter-finals.

Although I played in three of our League Cup matches and in our two opening league victories over Aberdeen and Motherwell, I barely featured in the first half of the campaign, losing my centre-half berth to Jock Paterson. Now in his tenth season at Easter Road, Jock had traditionally played at left-back, but he had spent the last couple of years jostling with me for the number five shirt. But first-team regular or not, I was delighted that by December we were up to second – behind Hearts – in the table. That's when – as it invariably did in those days – the rot set in. A miserable run of five straight defeats followed, plunging us back down to seventh and leaving the Scottish Cup as our last chance of collecting a trophy. A famous curse, indifferent form and common sense told us that there would be more chance of Lawrie Reilly buying a house in Gorgie than we had of giving our supporters their grand day out at Hampden Park.

And after our miserable experiences of recent years, there was little to suggest following a goalless draw at Tannadice against Dundee United that this campaign would be any different. Then again, in the previous season we didn't have Joe Baker. Joe scored his first goal of the competition in the replay, a 2-0 win at Easter Road, and he scored again in the next game, an extraordinary 5-5 draw in the league with St Mirren. It's a scoreline you don't see too often these days, but it wasn't uncommon back in the 1950s and certainly kept the Pools coupons interesting. Significantly for me, however, Willie MacFarlane had picked up an injury against the Saints. This meant Jock Paterson reverting to left-back and me re-entering the fray on 1 March 1958 – my first appearance for over three months – for an unforgettable last-16 cup tie against league leaders Hearts.

We weren't relishing the prospect of a trip to Tynecastle, but then no team would. At this point Hearts were 15 points clear of Rangers at the top of the table and a double was on the cards. Under their brilliant young captain, Dave Mackay, they had lost only twice all season. But it was their goalscoring that was truly frightening, they had already hit a century in the league. On two occasions they had found the net seven times, on another they had scored eight and, on three more days they had scored nine. But despite the outstanding scoring exploits of players like Jimmy Wardhaugh, Jimmy Murray and Alex Young, the man who made the difference in that cup tie was Joe Baker, who hit all four of our goals in a 4-3 win. For a player to score four goals away to such a great side, on such a big occasion, was remarkable. For a 17-year-old in his debut season it was scarcely believable. If ever there was a result that made us believe that this could finally be our year in the Scottish Cup, then this was it.

Joe scored two more in our quarter-final win over Third Lanark to help set up a semi-final clash with Rangers at Hampden. After a 2-2 draw, Hibs were leading 2-1 in the replay when Rangers thought they had equalised in the final minute. The referee rightly ruled, however, that Ralph Brand had punched the ball out of Lawrie Leslie's hand in the build-up to the goal. We would feel greater sympathy for them in a few weeks' time. All eyes were now focused on Hibs' first appearance in the Scottish Cup Final since 1947, but, before then, we would have to say farewell to one of the greatest players ever to wear the green and white shirt.

On 21 April 1958, Lawrie Reilly played the last of his 355 matches for Hibs. The only member of the Famous Five to be born in Edinburgh, he had scored 237 goals for the club and managed to clock up his 238th in his final appearance – a 3-1 win over Rangers at Easter Road. Although still able to find the net, Lawrie had announced his retirement earlier in the season. The knee injury he'd picked up on Scotland duty a couple of years earlier had ultimately ended his career at the age of 29. An operation at the beginning of the season, the kind that would be a routine keyhole surgery for a player today, wasn't enough to keep him on the football field and even I had to take it easy on him in training. He had been used sparingly throughout the season, making only 15 appearances – the same number as me, incidentally – and when he did play, he had moved to inside-right to accommodate Joe.

I didn't feature in the cup semi-finals but, on that cold Monday evening, I faced Rangers and then joined my team-mates and the opposition in a guard of honour to applaud Lawrie from the pitch. He had been made captain for the occasion, and the win and the goal – only his second of the season – was a fitting send-off to a true Hibs and Scotland great. We were now just five days from our date at Hampden, but even though I had featured in Lawrie's farewell, the chances of me running out at the national stadium looked unlikely. With the league campaign over for both clubs, the Rangers match had effectively been a testimonial and it was clear that, with the important business of the cup final now at hand, Jock Paterson would be the man to play at Hampden.

I had played quite a bit with Jock when he was at left-back and he was equally adept at centre-half. A big, friendly chap who was always full of advice for young players like me, he had played really well in the last-four clashes with Rangers, so I couldn't really have any argument. And so, just like the European Cup semi-final, it looked like I would be left to cheer on Hibs from the sidelines. On the morning of the match, Jock's name was there for all to see when the team was printed in the *Glasgow Herald*. It was also there in black and white in the official match programme, which my brother Robert, who was standing among the throngs of Hibs supporters at Hampden, read with disappointment. But that disappointment soon turned to joy when the Hibs players emerged from the tunnel and he spotted his big brother running on to the pitch. I think he was almost as surprised as I was.

Things happened so quickly that I don't remember the precise details; whether Jock had perhaps strained something, if he wasn't feeling well or if Hugh Shaw just had a last-minute change of heart. The point was that I was about to fulfil a boyhood dream – to play in the Scottish Cup Final. The noise was incredible as the deafening roar of nearly 100,000 supporters shook the stadium. I hadn't experienced anything like it since the Coronation Cup Final, but unlike this day, I had only been a spectator. More than 60 years later, I can still picture that moment perfectly and I can feel my pulse quicken just thinking about it. Much had been made of the fact that both Hibs and Clyde were going for their third Scottish Cup. But while Clyde last lifted the trophy in 1955, Hibs' most recent victory had been celebrated with a parade down Princes Street on a horse-drawn tram.

We also felt extra pressure given the fact that Hearts had so convincingly won the championship. Were we to triumph at Hampden, it would mark the first Edinburgh double of league and Scottish Cup since 1895, when Hearts won the title for the first time. Just to show how long ago it was since this had last happened, it wasn't even Hibs who had won the cup that year. That distinction belonged to another capital side, St Bernard's. At this point I'm imagining the dulcet tones of a young Scouser in a popular 1980s milk advert. 'St Bernard's? 'Oo are they?' Exactly. Leaving St Bernard's aside, there was a strong feeling among the press, at least in the west of Scotland, that – even with Joe Baker in our ranks – our Glasgow opponents were favourites to complete their Scottish Cup hat-trick first.

Clyde, too, had a forward on top form. Although he only joined them from Dundee United in the second half of the season, John Coyle was the most prolific striker in the country. Like Joe, he had so far scored seven goals in the Scottish Cup, including a hat-trick in Clyde's semi-final win over Motherwell. The romantics among the Scottish media had also speculated that Lawrie might appear for one last hurrah at Hampden, but a bout of tonsillitis meant that Hugh Shaw wasn't left with the difficult decision of leaving out either Andy Aitken or John

Fraser. Lawrie himself admitted that even if he had been fit his inclusion wouldn't have been fair. We did, however, have two players who had appeared in the 1947 final and we hoped that the experience of Eddie Turnbull and Willie Ormond, as well as the firepower of Joe Baker, would give us a good chance.

Having been on the losing side in two finals as a Hibs player, Hugh Shaw also felt that this might finally be his year. Whatever the talk of which side was going for however many trophies, who would play where and how they would play, the fact was that this was anybody's game. The day before the big match, Harry Swan predicted that it would be 'the best final since the war', adding, 'Both teams are playing great football. They are closely matched and the pitch at Hampden is in fine condition.' If Harry did have a crystal ball then he must have bought it on the cheap. The 95,000 supporters who packed into the stadium that day witnessed a match that, if I was being kind, I would refer to as 'not a classic'.

The Clyde captain Harry Haddock, perhaps eager to make up for Scotland's 4-0 defeat to England on the same pitch a few days earlier, won the toss and, unsurprisingly, chose to play with the wind in what turned out to be extremely blustery conditions. In the days before substitutions, we got off to a terrible start when Andy Aitken, who had scored in the first semi-final against Rangers, took a nasty knock after just quarter of an hour and hobbled about for the remainder of the game. Even the sceptics among us took one look at our stricken inside-right and thought that there might be something to this cup curse after all. English football fans had witnessed something similar during the previous season's FA Cup Final when Aston Villa's

Peter McParland collided with Manchester United goalkeeper Ray Wood. What was described by footballers of a certain era as 'a good old-fashioned shoulder charge' resulted in Jackie Blanchflower going in goal and Wood spending the rest of the match on the wing nursing a fractured cheekbone and suffering from concussion. Was it more of a man's game in those days? Possibly. But it could be a bit of a mug's game, too and Andy's injury certainly didn't help our cause.

Just before the half-hour, Coyle proved that things really were going all his way. The ball was cleared out of the Clyde defence and eventually made its way to him just inside the area. The in-form striker took aim as I slid in. He then miss-hit his shot but watched with delight as it deflected off John Baxter and into the net. It was his eighth goal of the competition and, despite never having previously represented Scotland at any level, that strike helped Coyle book a ticket to that summer's World Cup finals in Sweden. And though Scotland were clearly having trouble scoring, he failed to make a single appearance and was never selected for his country again. And England fans thought Theo Walcott was hard done by in 2006. But it showed the quality of that Clyde team that Coyle, along with Harry Haddock and Archie Robertson, went to the 1958 World Cup, while Eddie Turnbull was our sole representative.

Our fans thought we'd scored an equaliser late on but it was obvious, even from where I was standing, that Joe Baker had put hobbling Andy Aitken's cross into the net with his hand. We had come close but cigars were again in short supply. I got hold of a copy of the SFA's match programme afterwards. With a grim sense of prophecy, it read, 'Not solely by success is the fibre of men to be assessed. Hibs have had their victories, but better still, they have taken their reverses with a philosophic submission to fortune that might well be an example to others.' Try telling that to the flower pot I gave what for to when I got home that night.

Hibs wouldn't appear in the Scottish Cup Final again until 1972, when Eddie Turnbull had taken over as manager. The 6-1 thrashing of his Tornadoes at the hands of Celtic was followed in 1979 by an agonising defeat to Rangers, who needed three matches and an own goal to finally claim victory. The agony continued – if sporadically – over the next three and half decades, with three more cup final defeats to come before that glorious, unforgettable day in 2016. When one defeat turns into three in a row, then four, then seven, the mental pressure adds an enormous weight to the physical strain of winning an important match.

If Hibs could look anywhere for inspiration then it was to one of their most famous fans, Andy Murray, who lost his first five Grand Slam tennis finals before finally getting the monkey off his back at the 2012 US Open. For those Hibs players who took on Rangers at Hampden Park four years later, it wasn't so much a monkey on their backs but an entire planet of apes. I know I speak for every Hibs supporter when I say that I hope we don't have to wait another 114 years to win it again. Winning is something that takes discipline, something that, at the time of my ultimately disappointing experience at Hampden, I was now learning a whole lot more about.

7

A Private Captain

OF ALL the sociopaths, miscreants and misfits who colour the pages of Joseph Heller's great anti-war novel *Catch-22*, perhaps the most tragic is Major Major Major Major. The character was doomed from the moment of his birth when his father, Mr Major, rushed from the hospital to register his infant son's first and middle names as Major and Major.

So when Major Major Major joined the US Army, he rose quickly through the ranks but was destined never to go any further than that of major, his superiors' sense of humour being every bit as twisted as his dad's. As though that wasn't bad enough, an unfortunate resemblance to Henry Fonda had seen Major Major Major Major spend his life apologising to people because he wasn't actually the Oscar-winning actor.

I don't think I've ever been mistaken for a movie star and I never planned to be in the British Army long enough to rise to the rank of major, but I could later empathise with the confusion surrounding the character. From the moment I signed up, I was Private John Plenderleith of the Royal Army Service Corps, but when I was made captain of the British Army football team, I was listed as Driver John Plenderleith. My commanding officer felt that turning a lowly private into a captain – even if it was just on the football field – might put some officers' noses out of joint. As far as I was concerned, though, he could call me what he liked, as long as I got to play. I did actually reach the level of Staff Sergeant, but I held that rank purely within the confines of Holytown Boys' Brigade and I don't think it would hold much sway on the battlefield.

I had no particular desire to become a soldier but, like so many other young men at the time, I wasn't given a choice. In the 1940s, after thousands of men and women who had served in the forces during the Second World War had been demobilised (or demobbed) and had re-entered civilian life, the British Government was conscious that it still needed plenty of military manpower to help protect the country's interests abroad. After all, that rapidly dwindling number of overseas territories it called an empire wasn't going to look after itself.

Passed by Clement Attlee's Labour government in 1947 and coming into effect in January 1949, the National Service Act meant that all physically fit men aged between 17 and 21 were required to serve in one of the armed forces for 18 months, after which they would stay on the reserve list for another four years.

In 1950, a further National Service Act saw the 18-month period extended to two years, with national servicemen taking part in various operations in places like Korea, Cyprus and Kenya. National Service was far from popular, especially following six years of war, and was seen to impact on the economy at a time when the country could barely afford it. The

Act was scrapped in 1960 and the last of the national servicemen were discharged in 1963.

But amid the negativity, the requirement for all those young men to serve two years in the forces had at least one thing going for it: the National Service years were described by the British Army as being a 'memorable epoch' in Army football. A quick roll-call of just a few of my Army team-mates will give you an idea why: Lance Corporal Gerry Hitchens (Aston Villa, Inter Milan and England); Lance Corporal Peter Dobing (Blackburn Rovers, Manchester City and Stoke); Private Alex Young (Hearts, Everton and Scotland); Sapper Davie Wilson (Rangers, Dundee United and Scotland); Fusilier Alex Parker (Everton, Falkirk and Scotland); and Private John Barnwell (Arsenal and Nottingham Forest).

In some ways we felt like a team of ringers. The fact that so many professional footballers were in the ranks didn't give the other soldiers much of a look-in when it came to representing the Army on the football pitch, a bit like that episode of *The Simpsons* when Homer loses his place on the softball team after his boss, Mr Burns, hires a bunch of Major League Baseball stars to work at the nuclear power plant. At the same time, we were young men who just wanted to do what we did best.

The call to sign up wasn't unexpected. I knew that, as soon as I had finished my joinery apprenticeship, I would be required to do my bit for Queen and Country. I was still keen to play for Hibs so I hoped that, like Alex Scott of Rangers, I might be fortunate enough to be based at Edinburgh Castle – now that would have been handy. In the end, being stationed with the RASC in Hampshire could have been worse. I'd have had trouble making it to Easter Road every Saturday if I'd been stationed somewhere like Cyprus. And my weekend commute was nothing compared to that of one of my former team-mates. During his own National Service years, goalkeeper Tommy Younger used to turn out for Hibs virtually every weekend despite being based in Germany. British European Airways even presented him with a plaque for making more than 100 flights. I'm not sure that Dennis Bergkamp, the non-flying Dutchman, would have managed to fulfil his club commitments under similar circumstances.

* * *

Although most of the time I would travel by train to Edinburgh, I would sometimes fly back to Scotland, but I was never in any danger of accumulating the same number of air miles as Tommy. I was fortunate that my commanding officer at 3 Training Battalion in Farnborough was a big football fan and he would always go out of his way to make sure I could be available for Hibs. This was provided, of course, that it didn't stop me turning out for the Army team. I would walk to a payphone and call Easter Road on a Friday to say that I would be available the next day. One of these occasions, thankfully, included the 1958 Scottish Cup Final. Our Hibs goalkeeper, Lawrie Leslie, who was stationed with the Royal Artillery, didn't always find his commanders so accommodating. He missed quite a few games for the club, while I managed to make around 50 appearances for them during my two years in the Army.

Those of us who were selected to play for the British Army side were required to get an availability slip signed by our commanding officer – it was a bit like getting your parents to sign a form to allow you to go on a school trip. It certainly felt like that sometimes, and we had plenty of laughs while on the road. Of course, it wasn't convenient as far as my football career was concerned. After a couple of seasons spent in and out of the side, I had reached a stage where I really wanted to establish myself as a first-team regular at Easter Road. The last thing I needed was to be sent to the south of England for two years, but all young players were in the same boat. Football and the Army go back a long way and I knew that, compared to the horrific experiences of some players during wartime, those who had to fit their club matches round National Service had it easy.

Being tackled by someone like Dave Mackay was hardly a walk in the park but it was nothing compared to being in the trenches. Everyone knows the story of the British and German soldiers having a game in no man's land during the Christmas Day truce of 1914. This inspired, among many other things, a brilliant line in *Blackadder Goes Forth*. Asked whether he remembers the football match, Rowan Atkinson's Captain Blackadder replies, 'Remember it? How could I forget it? I was never offside. I could not *believe* that decision!'

Alongside the semi-mythical status of the Yuletide kickabout, there are numerous stories of tragedy and heroism among football's soldiers. Hearts, for example, were the first British side to sign up to the First World War en masse. Of the 16 players who went to the front line, three died on the first day of the Battle of the Somme, four died elsewhere in battle and several of the nine who made it home had suffered wounds so severe that they were never able to play football again.

But despite the memorials to those players who had made such sacrifices during the first global conflict, it seemed that the football authorities still had difficulty reading the public mood. Shortly before top-flight football was cancelled following the outbreak of the Second World War, Cowdenbeath defender George Jordan enlisted in the Black Watch regiment and, within days, several of his team-mates had also signed up and it left the Fife club unable to field a team. One would assume that the Scottish Football League would show understanding to the club and be grateful to its footballers for being prepared to fight for their country. Instead, Cowdenbeath were slapped with a £500 fine. The mind boggles and, unsurprisingly, it's a penalty that still rankles among the Fifers some 80 years later. Cowdenbeath were forced to sell one of their players to St Mirren in order to pay the fine, while Jordan was killed at Normandy in 1944 at the age of 27.

* * *

By the time I was representing the Army team, there seemed to be a greater feeling of mutual respect between the forces and clubs. Ahead of our match against a Scotland XI in 1958, John Park, the SFA president, said, 'I should like to take this opportunity of expressing to the Army authorities, on behalf of the clubs, appreciation of their willingness to release players for club duty, Saturday after Saturday, whenever practicable. We, in Scotland, are most grateful for this continued consideration.'

The Army authorities, too, were grateful to the clubs and national sides for providing their players with strong opposition. Sometimes it worked out for both teams. Turning out for the

Army against an FA XI at St James' Park in Newcastle in October 1959 also gave me the chance to play for Hibs in a friendly against Bolton Wanderers at Easter Road. In between drills and marches and playing football for the Army, my battalion and for Hibs, I worked as a physical training instructor at Farnborough. If I thought I was in good shape when I used to play all those matches as a teenager, it was nothing compared to my level of fitness while I was in the Army. The Duracell bunny had nothing on me.

As well as lining up with some great players, we also came up against a few, but the schedule could be hectic. As well as playing against club sides – including Rangers, Everton and Aberdeen – we'd play international XIs, and we'd also come up against other Army teams. Some of us would find ourselves in the unusual position of playing our own clubs at grounds we'd normally call home. Having beaten Hibs 6-1 in a Monday night friendly at Easter Road, I then played *for* Hibs in their 2-1 win against Clyde that Saturday. During this period, I was also playing for Scotland Under-23s and I even captained a Hibs-Hearts combined XI against the Army, so it was easy to forget which kit you were supposed to be wearing.

It was a bit disorienting, especially after a long train journey, reporting to Easter Road to play against Hibs, or turning up at Tynecastle to play in the same side as Hearts players. I had made a few trips to Gorgie during my Hibs career, some successful, others less so, but my biggest defeat there came while captaining the Army. My Easter Road team-mate John Fraser was also in the side that lost 8-1, while Gordon Smith was among those to find the net for the hosts. What was frightening is that Hearts managed to put on such a high-scoring display without their superb marksman, Alex Young. That's because, unfortunately for the young private on that occasion, he was playing for us.

Being in the Army was a great chance to meet and swap experiences with other players, not just at home but abroad. Recognised by FIFA as the oldest cup competition in Europe, the triangular tournament that became known as the Kentish Cup was first contested in 1921 in the hope that it would foster relations between armed forces. Up until 1986, when France withdrew and were replaced by the Netherlands, the tournament was held between the respective armies of Britain, France and Belgium. The 1958/59 competition kicked off on 14 December 1958 when I was selected to represent the 'Armée Britannique' against the Armée Française in Paris. I remember we were instructed to wear uniform throughout our journey to France, with only officers being permitted to wear 'civvies'. Not that this applied to any of the players, none of whom ranked higher than Lance Corporal.

Winning the Kentish Cup would put the British Army out in front with 11 victories, ahead of Belgium with ten and France on nine. It was a great honour to be part of such an historic tournament and I was even more thrilled because, following the disappointment of missing out in the European Cup semi-final against Reims, it meant I would finally get to play at the Parc des Princes. But, as is so often the case, the match failed to live up to the occasion.

Desmond Hackett, the distinctive, bowler hat-wearing football correspondent from the *Daily Express*, singled me out for special praise, encouraging Arsenal – who had expressed interest in signing me – to 'make a quick, open-cheque bid or they will miss out on one of the greatest centre-halves since John Charles'. That was an amazing compliment. He was also of the opinion, however, that the British Army team had 'achieved the incredible feat of making my lovely Paris look drab' during our 2-1 defeat. I suppose sometimes you have to take the rough with the smooth.

Ironically, given that it was two teams of soldiers doing battle, the game didn't offer much in the way of attacking football and there were plenty of whistles and jeers around the stadium as the match failed to ignite. Finally, on 70 minutes, the home crowd had something to cheer when Newcastle's Bill McKinney hauled down Maryan Wisniewski – at that point the youngest man ever to represent France – and the Lens striker scrambled the ball into the net following the free kick. Gerry Hitchens nodded in an equaliser a minute later, only for François Heutte – who would represent his country at the European Championships in 1960 – to score the winner with probably the only decent shot of the game. There was at least one consolation after losing – the roast lamb, champagne and liqueurs we enjoyed in the post-match banquet were a damn sight tastier than anything we were served up in the mess back home.

I was reminded of playing for the Army in Paris one Sunday afternoon when *Escape to Victory* came on the television. The movie sees an Allied prisoners of war team consisting of – among others – Michael Caine, Sylvester Stallone, Bobby Moore and Pelé, take on the Nazis in the French capital. Their original plan is to leg it at half-time through a tunnel La Resistance has dug into their dressing room. But, sensing they can defy the odds and the biased referee, they re-emerge for the second half and – thanks to an overhead kick from Pelé and a last-minute penalty save from Sly – they manage to secure a 4-4 draw before disappearing into the Parisian crowd. Utterly ludicrous, of course, but entertaining, although strictly speaking it should have been called *Escape to Draw*.

France eventually won that year's Kentish Cup and, in 1980, the British Army handed the tournament over to the Combined Services Football Association. With military conscription still active in Belgium, meaning they still fielded professionals, it was felt that the Brits needed to widen their pool of players. Things certainly didn't seem as straightforward when they didn't have some of the country's best young footballers in their ranks.

Before the disappointment of Paris, we had put in a far better performance a month earlier against a Scotland XI put together by Matt Busby. It had been nearly a decade since the Army had last played a Scotland team. On that day, Rangers' Willie Waddell had, in the words of the secretary of the Army Football Association, given the soldiers 'a tantalising run-around not easily forgotten' during a 7-1 tanking. The side we were up against looked to be equally strong, with their line-up including Dave Mackay, who had followed up captaining Hearts to the league championship with victory in the League Cup, Eric Caldow of Rangers, and a skinny young inside-left from Huddersfield Town named Denis Law.

Busby, who had so nearly lost his life in Munich at the beginning of the year, had handed Law his first Scotland cap against Wales just a few weeks earlier and it was easy to see why the 18-year-old was being talked about with such excitement both north and south of the border. It took the Law Man – or should I say the Law Boy – just over three minutes to get on the scoresheet at Tynecastle. After being humbled 4-1 by a Football Association XI in our previous match, however, we played well and salvaged a draw through Gerry Hitchens.

Having, at that point, represented my country at schools, Under-18 and Under-23 level, I have to admit that it felt a little bit strange to be playing against Scotland, although it wasn't as peculiar as the situation my Hibs club-mate Joe Baker found himself in – playing against Scotland in the colours of England despite growing up in Lanarkshire. I felt far more at home playing against the FA Select at St James' Park, where I came up against another prolific young goalscorer – Brian Clough of Middlesbrough, who was averaging a goal a game at club level. Although he scored with a superb effort from a corner, I received praise for managing to keep him contained for the majority of the match. I'm not dropping any bombshells by saying that Clough was big-headed, but he was also brilliant, and how he and Joe accumulated only ten England caps between them I'll never know.

During those two years I played a lot of matches, competitive and friendly, for several different sides. I learned a lot about transporting supplies during wartime, but I was grateful for never having to fire a shot in anger. Towards the end of my first year in the Army, Anne and I were married in Holytown. It was Christmas Eve 1958. We planned to buy a house in Edinburgh and, after working as a joiner and after another year in the Army, I would finally have the chance to become a full-time footballer for Hibs. But sometimes life takes you in a different – and entirely unexpected – direction.

8

End of the Easter Road

THERE'S ALWAYS been a lot of talk about boys becoming men in the Army. I don't know if that's any more true than in other professions but, certainly, a lot changed in my life – and at Hibs – during my two years of National Service. Although we now had quite a youthful side, our appearance in the Scottish Cup Final gave us confidence that we could have another good run in the competition in the 1958/59 season. We managed to set up a quarter-final tie at Third Lanark, the team which would famously go out of business in 1967, with wins over Falkirk and Partick Thistle. But a brace from Dave Hilley, who would later play for Newcastle United and Nottingham Forest, meant there would be no quick return to Hampden Park for Hibs or our thousands of dedicated fans.

Even those who travelled to Glasgow to watch us fall to Third Lanark didn't have an entirely wasted journey. It wouldn't become clear until the end of the season, but that 2-1 defeat marked the last of Gordon Smith's 636 appearances for the club. Had Gordon decided to hang up his boots at that point, he would have left behind a tremendous footballing legacy. The fact he didn't ended up paving the way for one of the most remarkable stories in the history of the game.

Suffering from a recurring ankle injury, Gordon knew that he would need surgery in order to prolong his career. Despite Hugh Shaw fighting his corner, it was an operation that Harry Swan and the Hibs board decided they weren't prepared to pay for. So they cut their losses, gave Gordon a free transfer and then showed him the exit. Perhaps spurred on by the club's attitude, Gordon decided to pay for the surgery out of his own pocket – possibly still making his way through that wad of ten-bob notes he produced at Aberdeen railway station – and moved across Edinburgh to join Hearts. He won another league title at Tynecastle, as well as the League Cup before – at the age of 37 – he was again thought to have reached his sell-by date. But Gordon's Indian Summer didn't end there as Dundee manager Bob Shankly felt there was enough left in the Smith tank to bring him to Dens Park. Playing alongside future Spurs legend Alan Gilzean, not only did the veteran winger earn yet another league championship medal but he also helped Dundee reach the semi-final of the European Cup – seven years after reaching the same stage of the competition with Hibs.

There are plenty of inspirational tales in football, players who have overcome age and injury, teams which were never given a chance yet defied all the odds, but I rate the odyssey of Gordon Smith above all others. To win three league championships with three different clubs is a remarkable feat in any country, but to do it in Scotland, having played for neither Rangers or Celtic, is truly amazing. Manchester United's treble win of 1999 was superb, but I think one day it could be done again. I don't think

I'm sticking my neck out when I say that Gordon's treble of three Scottish league championships with three non-Old Firm clubs will never be repeated. As for Harry Swan, writing off Gordon by failing to stick his hand in his pocket suggested he was still putting his faith in the crystal ball he'd used to predict a classic cup final between us and Clyde.

At the end of that 1958/59 season, we also said farewell – although not goodbye – to yet another member of the Famous Five. Eddie Turnbull, who I'd played with on more than 100 occasions, retired as a player and stepped into the role of trainer, first of the reserves and then of the first team. As well as being a terrific player and a hugely loyal servant to Hibs, Eddie had always been a vocal and commanding presence at the club. His new role suited him perfectly and started him off on a successful managerial career with Aberdeen and, of course, Hibs. My idea of a Turnbull Tornado was the way he would rip into me if I ever made a mistake, but he could also be very supportive and he certainly knew his football. I would still get the odd bollocking but his retirement as a player meant my ears were at least given a rest during games.

We ended up finishing tenth in the league, while, in a title race that came down to the last day of the season, Rangers pipped Hearts to what would have been their second championship in a row.

The new champions ensured we suffered another abysmal start to the 1959/60 season, beating us 6-1 at home in the League Cup. Lawrie Leslie's continued recovery from an operation on his elbow meant that Jackie Wren played in goal. Ralph Brand scored four times and Hugh Shaw called ours a 'lacklustre display' in front of 45,000 supporters. We fared only slightly better at Ibrox, losing 5-1. And defeats in our other four matches, home and away to Dundee and to Motherwell, meant that I would never experience playing in a Scottish League Cup quarter-final. Over at Tynecastle, meanwhile, a veteran winger named Gordon Smith was on his way to a winner's medal.

It wasn't just Brand who enjoyed scoring against us. After going into the lead in our home tie against Motherwell, a 21-year-old local lad settled the match in a dizzyingly short space of time. If you'd had the misfortune – or fortune, depending on which side you were supporting – of nipping to the toilet between the 78th and 81st minutes, you'd have missed one of the quickest hat-tricks in the history of senior football. Ian St John's two and a half minutes of brilliance helped cement his reputation as one of the country's top young strikers and, two seasons later, he would be off to Liverpool. Even though I had a good write-up after that game, in the *Motherwell Times* of all newspapers, I had to put up with banter from the Army lads for several months afterwards, with the refrain of 'St John's going to get you'. Oh, how I laughed, especially the 50th time I heard it.

But we had a prolific young Lanarkshire striker of our own in Joe Baker. With him in the side, we knew we'd always have a chance, and this was the season he would go on to score 46 goals in only 42 appearances. He ensured our league campaign got off to a great start by netting a brace in a 2-1 win over Aberdeen. He then scored two more in a 2-2 draw with Hearts at Tynecastle. I remember this match for a few other reasons: the rock-hard surface that meant only those who didn't value the skin on their legs would brave a sliding tackle; the fact our old friend Gordon

Smith managed to sky a late opportunity to score the winner over the bar; and the searing pain I suffered as the result of a good old-fashioned groin injury. I can confirm that it's every bit as sore as it sounds, and I had to delay my return to barracks until the Tuesday evening. It was touch and go whether I would be fit to play Rangers in the league that weekend, but in the end, I was given the nod. Compared to the usual 40,000-plus we got for matches against the Old Firm, it was a disappointing crowd of only 25,000 – the majority in light blue scarves – who turned up at Easter Road. But then, when you've seen your side ship 11 goals to the same opposition in the space of a month, it was difficult to blame them. We must have been improving, though, as only a Jimmy Millar goal for Rangers 12 minutes from time could separate us.

One thing I will say about Hugh Shaw, and I should know more than most, is that he wasn't afraid to give youth a chance. In goal against Rangers was 17-year-old Willie Wilson, who had been handed his debut in our League Cup defeat to Dundee, displacing Jackie Wren following the 6-1 hammering in our opening game. At the other end of the pitch, we had Joe Baker, who had only turned 19 in July. At just shy of my 22nd birthday, I already felt like a veteran. But while our manager was clearly looking to the future, he also had an eye on the past. During the summer he had brought Bobby Johnstone back from Manchester City, where he was a firm fan favourite and made history by becoming the first player to score in successive FA Cup Finals at Wembley.

There was no doubt that his signing gave us a bit of a lift and he made his second debut for Hibs in our 4-2 win over

Kilmarnock. He would have to play a few more games before he was reunited with fellow Famous Five alumnus Willie Ormond against Dunfermline on 17 October, a match which kick-started a season full of truly extraordinary results. Although Joe Baker scored a hat-trick, Bobby pulled a lot of the strings in our 7-4 win. Joe scored another three a week later when we beat Airdrie 11-1 at Broomfield Park. For once, Joe was eclipsed in the goalscoring stakes as Tommy Preston got four. It's still a Scottish record for an away win in the league and it wasn't the only time we reached double figures that season. We also ran riot against Partick Thistle, beating them 10-2 at Firhill on 19 December. It's a thrill to be part of a side which is capable of producing those kind of performances, where everything seems to go right, every pass reaches its intended recipient and virtually every shot finds the net. These were the sorts of results you'd be surprised to see on a school playground let alone in Division One. But it was clear that we were still frail defensively, including in a 6-6 draw in a friendly with Middlesbrough.

We lost successive games on Boxing Day and New Year's Day, 6-4 away to Aberdeen and then, even worse, 5-1 at home to Hearts. Following the Hogmanay thrashing at Tynecastle during my first season, this was the second time I'd played in a 5-1 defeat in a New Year derby. This time felt even worse from a personal point of view because, although I finally managed to get on the scoresheet, it was for Hearts. We were a goal down to the league leaders after just seven minutes and, under pressure from Alex Young, I jumped up to try to clear a spinning ball that had been flicked on by Bobby Blackwood. It skidded off the top of my head and wrong-footed Jackie Wren, who could

END OF THE EASTER ROAD

only watch it trickle over the line. If you're ever having a bad day at work, just try to imagine scoring an own goal for your local rivals in front of 54,000 supporters at your own ground – on Hogmanay. Young got a hat-trick and Gordon Smith, having a ball at his new club, scored Hearts' fifth. It's no wonder that Hibs fans took such delight in the match on New Year's Day in 1973 – a 7-0 win at Tynecastle.

Most footballers will tell you that, after a bad result, the next game can't come quickly enough. It's all about getting back in the saddle and trying to make amends to the team, to the fans and to yourself. Hibs didn't have to wait long as they were due to play at Ibrox the very next day, but I discovered that I would have to wait a little longer. Along with Jackie, I was unceremoniously dropped for the match against Rangers. While Jackie was replaced in goal by debutant Willie Muirhead, an apprentice joiner brought in from Arniston Rangers, my place went to Pat Hughes. On the face of it, we couldn't complain too much about Hugh Shaw's decision because the 1-1 draw with second-place Rangers restored some respectability, albeit with the unintended consequence of pushing Hearts slightly closer to the league title.

Unlike the day he called me into his office as a 17-year-old to tell me that he was planning to 'rest' me, Hugh didn't bother breaking out the kid gloves for an old man of 22. Before home games, you only found out whether you were playing when the manager pinned the team sheet on the dressing room door. It was only just as I was leaving that he told me he wouldn't be requiring my services in Glasgow. I suppose he at least had the decency to tell me before I turned up at Ibrox. Hugh is rightly held up as a legendary Hibs manager, but I don't think he got everything right.

He used to take us for pre-season training sessions at Gullane beach, which is about 20 miles down what is now known as 'Scotland's Golf Coast' in East Lothian. It's a lovely place for a round of golf, but Hugh would make us run up and down the sand dunes. This was long before Jock Wallace hit the headlines by employing similar tactics with Berwick Rangers. The player-manager put his side's shock 1967 Scottish Cup win over Rangers down to his team's stamina, and he later put players like Ally McCoist through their paces at Gullane when he was manager at Ibrox. Hugh didn't push us as hard as Wallace, with tales of players throwing up on their shirts and still being made to run, but I thought the whole exercise was bloody stupid.

I knew the principle was that if you could run fast on sand then you could run even faster on the pitch, but we were using our muscles in a completely different way to how we used them when playing football. All it did was make our legs ache and our tempers short. As far as I was concerned, football training should always be done with a football. I remember reading about Arrigo Sacchi, manager of the great AC Milan side of the late 1980s and early 1990s, conducting a training session which consisted of his squad playing a full 90-minute 'match' without the ball. This supposedly helped with their positioning. I know it's difficult for me to argue given that Sacchi won numerous trophies while at Milan, but I refuse to believe players like Marco Van Basten and Ruud Gullit would have wanted to do anything other than have the ball at their feet. It's why we play the game. I know it sounds big-headed, but when I was a young player, I think I could control the ball just about as well as any other player out there. That's because I spent as many hours as I could with a ball. If a football wasn't available, then I'd use a tennis ball, or even a golf ball. As far as I can see, the only advantage of me playing a match without a ball would be that I might finally get on the scoresheet. I would just turn away with my arms in the air claiming I'd just hit a 35-yard screamer into the top corner.

But while I didn't enjoy struggling up and down the sand dunes in East Lothian, I did have some fun on the links course. If we'd had a particularly good game on a Saturday, then Hugh would let us play golf there on a Monday morning. I had never picked up a golf club before I went to Hibs, but Lawrie Reilly and Gordon Smith, in particular, were big fans of the game. I picked it up reasonably quickly and still play golf today, although I probably spend about as much time in the sand as I did during pre-season training on the dunes. To make things more interesting we would all put money in a kitty, with the prize going to the man who played the best round. One day, we were in the middle of playing and it started to rain. It continued to get heavier and showed no signs of stopping. One by one, the Hibs players called it a day and headed back to the clubhouse for a drink. All except me – the pig-headed teenager. Wind howling and cold rain lashing my face, I ploughed on alone. An hour or so later I squelched into the clubhouse, water dripping off my clothes and on to the plush carpet. Lawrie stared at me in disbelief, a drink frozen halfway to his lips.

'Where in god's name have you been, Jackie? We all packed up ages ago.'

'I know,' I grinned. 'I was the only one who finished the round, now where's my money?'

They laughed and coughed up the cash, but it was the only time I ever took home the kitty. As well as sharing so many good times on the football pitch, that was one of the many precious memories I had of playing for Hibs, which made me regret the fact that my time at Easter Road might be coming to an end, particularly with Pat Hughes retaining his place in the side. I was out of the team for the next four matches, only coming back in after Pat was injured in a 5-5 draw with Clyde.

I enjoyed a successful return, a 4-3 win over Motherwell, thanks to late goals from Willie Ormond and Tommy Preston, and then played in our successive 3-0 Scottish Cup victories over Dundee and East Stirlingshire. In a season full of cricket scores, these were only our second and third clean sheets of the entire campaign and they paved the way for a hard-fought – and at times bad-tempered – quarter-final against Rangers at Ibrox. The referee immediately made himself unpopular with the fervent home support when he awarded us a penalty for handball after just two minutes. Bobby Johnstone tucked it away, only for Sammy Baird to equalise just before half-time. Davie Wilson put Rangers ahead with a free kick, but we refused to lie down and Johnny MacLeod – who would later score Arsenal's very first goal in European competition – brought us level during a goalmouth scramble. It took a brilliant strike from Jimmy Millar to settle the tie and dash our hopes of reaching a second successive cup final. In a match full of a heavy challenges, it was also one of the few times in my career that I had my name taken by the referee. I could be a hard tackler but I was also very clean. The fact I went in the book was perhaps an indication of my desire to win and to stay in the manager's plans.

I did, but only for another two matches. I played in successive defeats at Easter Road, 3-1 to St Mirren and then 3-0 to Raith Rovers. Of course I had already experienced the sting of being dropped after losing to Raith and, after playing my heart out against Rangers, seeing Pat's name on the team sheet to face Dundee really hurt. Nevertheless, I was prepared to live with it and fight for my place. But when – after the 6-3 defeat to Dundee – the centre-half berth went to Joe McClelland and then to John Young, I decided I'd had enough.

I never had any desire to leave the club. Shortly after my National Service came to an end in late January, Anne and I had bought our first house together in Corstorphine. Living so close to Murrayfield, Tommy Preston said it would be really handy for watching Scotland play England in the 1960 Five Nations Championship. But I had absolutely no interest in watching rugby, I only wanted to play football. After being demobbed I decided to put the joinery on hold and become a full-time professional. If having the chance to play regularly meant leaving Edinburgh, having only just moved house, then I would give it serious thought. But there was more to it. In the run-up to Christmas 1959, Anne and I were thrilled to find out that we were going to be parents. Perhaps it was impending fatherhood that gave me a different perspective on things – a greater sense of pride, or maybe stubbornness. Whatever it was, I didn't make my next move on a whim.

Back then, clubs owned players to an extent that would horrify today's professionals, some of whom are able to hold a team to ransom in order to get a couple more zeros added to their weekly wages. In my era, there was no waiting for your contract to expire and then leaving on a free transfer. You were contracted to the club for your career. They held all the aces and, if they decided they didn't want to sell you, then that was tough, you could stay in the reserves. In other words, handing in a transfer request wasn't the kind of thing you did lightly.

But I'd been playing for Hibs since I was 17. I was still only 22 and I'd managed to rack up 158 competitive appearances in addition to all those Floodlit Challenge matches. And despite being based in the south of England, I'd busted a gut to make sure I was available every weekend during my National Service. Now it seemed that no sooner had I been demobbed, turned full-time and bought a house in Edinburgh with my pregnant wife than I was being told I was now the fourth-choice centre-half.

I had enjoyed some amazing highs at Easter Road: Europe, the Scottish Cup Final, the win over Hearts, playing alongside amazing players like the Famous Five and Joe Baker. I'd also experienced a few lows, but that's life. That's football. I would always support Hibs, but it was time to move on. And so I put my request into writing and was promptly told that it was being turned down. The next day, the board issued a statement to say that I was 'ill-advised' to put in my transfer request and that a friendly chat would 'smooth things over'. I don't know if that friendly chat ever took place, but I was told that, although my request was being denied, they would be prepared to sell me if any club showed interest, which sounded like the same thing to me. I had taken a chance, and all I could do now was wait and see what happened and hope that I didn't end up in footballing limbo. Things had changed a lot in my five and a half seasons at Easter Road. Of the players who started my final match against Raith Rovers, only two – John Grant and Bobby Johnstone – were at the club when I made my debut, and Bobby had been down to Manchester in between.

I didn't know it when I walked off the pitch against Raith, but I was about to follow in Bobby's footsteps.

9

City Life

PELÉ WAS a genius on the football field. There can never be any argument about that but, like so many other fans of the game, I had a few issues with the FIFA 100. Unveiled in 2004 to celebrate the federation's centenary, this was a list of who were supposedly the greatest 125 living footballers and, like any such compilation, it wasn't met with universal acclaim. Dutch striker Marco Van Basten refused to have anything to do with it on principle, Pelé's former team-mate Gérson tore it up in disgust, and many of us were left shaking our heads in disbelief at the names of some of the players Pelé had chosen – or at least who he hadn't chosen. It was obvious that he'd been made to ensure a geographical spread to keep FIFA's various member states happy, but doing so led to some truly baffling omissions. I could devote a chapter to who I think should have been shoo-ins, so I'll keep it to two cast-iron certainties. And don't worry, I'm not among them. The first is John Charles, and I know there will be many thousands, especially in Turin, Leeds and in Wales, who will agree with me. The second is Denis Law. Pelé found room for only one

Scotsman on his list: Kenny Dalglish. I would never call for Kenny to be squeezed out, but there is no way that the man whose statue stands outside Old Trafford alongside Sir Bobby Charlton and George Best – both of whom made the list, incidentally – should have been left out.

I'd had the pleasure of captaining Denis for the Scotland Under-23s and had played against him for the British Army and it was obvious he was a cut above most other players on the park. The thing was that Denis knew it, something I discovered during a Manchester City training session. We were taking part in the kind of match we used to have at Easter Road – forwards versus defenders – and, of course, there was a bit of contact. Everyone knew that Denis could be a hard tackler himself, but when I got him and the ball, he went in the huff and our Scottish manager Les McDowall gave me a row for tackling him. Nobody showed me any pity when I got a crack, but, I suppose, I wasn't British football's record signing. In all seriousness, though, the chance to play in the same team as players like Denis helped make it an easy decision to join City.

Reading that I was unsettled at Easter Road, Les had made the approach at the end of June 1960 and, following a discussion between all parties that went on into the night, I was signed on 1 July in a deal worth around £17,500. It wasn't quite the £55,000 City had splashed out to bring Denis to Maine Road from Huddersfield Town, but nor was it peanuts for a defender. Indeed, the manager said that the money spent on me, Denis and on Barrie Betts from Stockport County was 'an outward and obvious sign of the club's determination to build a successful team'.

I knew City had been struggling for a couple of seasons, narrowly avoiding relegation to the Second Division during the previous campaign. But the money they were spending – although nowhere near the level of the multi-million pound sky blue empire of today – showed that they meant business. It was also an exciting prospect for me to play in England. I had played alongside a lot of English players during my national service and I'd also come up against quite a few English clubs in Floodlit Challenge matches. This included sharing a pitch with Dave Ewing in Hibs' floodlight friendly victory over City in 1955.

Originally from Perthshire, Dave had played at the heart of the City defence for the best part of a decade and he was a huge presence at the club in manner as well as in size. Although John McTavish had played at centre-half for most of the previous season, Dave had returned to help City in their fight against relegation. As he was now 31, however, I was brought in as Dave's replacement, but he was the complete professional, despite the circumstances, and we got on fine in training. We both accepted that it was neither his fault, nor mine, and we just got on with it. I also had the privilege at Maine Road of playing alongside Bert Trautmann, the former prisoner of war turned goalkeeper and national treasure most famous for his heroics in the 1956 FA Cup Final when he helped City beat Birmingham despite suffering a broken neck. I was great friends with Bert, but my best pal in Manchester was David Shawcross, the 19-year-old wing-half. It was partly because we played next to each other and partly because, like me, he had been thrust into first-team football at such a young age. Mostly, however, David was just a great guy to hang around with and we hit it off straight away.

During my first few months at Maine Road, I gave an interview with *Soccer Star* magazine, where I said I was enjoying life at Manchester City because I was able to play 'my natural style', whereas Hibs wanted me to be more of a 'stopper' centre-half in the mould of Dave Ewing, who could terrorise a striker just by looking at him. I certainly felt I was playing with a lot more freedom and, as a result, felt more at ease. The article added, 'With his natural attacking ability, [Jackie] is always on the look-out for a chance to get his attack going, and he never makes the mistake of going too far upfield, leaving a gap [thank you, Eddie!]. Take a look at City's goal average, and you'll see they have one of the best defensive records in Division One.'

We certainly got off to a decent start, drawing 2-2 at Nottingham Forest before enjoying consecutive wins over defending champions Burnley. The Lancashire club had secured the league title by beating City in the final game of the previous season, and I have to admit we were slightly fortunate in the first of these victories. Burnley had taken the lead at a sodden Maine Road after just five minutes, but Colin Barlow and Joe Hayes scored late goals while one of Burnley's star players, John Connelly, was off the pitch receiving treatment. But there was no doubt about the 3-1 victory at Turf Moor, which saw Denis Law at his brilliant best, running half the length of the pitch before firing in from the edge of the area. We were pleased with the win, but I also had something else on my mind at the time.

The following day – 31 August – I received word in training that, back in Bellshill, Anne had given birth to a healthy baby boy. I know many of today's fathers will be shocked to learn that I wasn't there when my son came in to the world, but it wasn't as common in those days and chances are I would just have got myself in the way. As soon as training was over, I asked Les if I could drive back to Scotland to see my wife and meet my newborn son. Permission was granted, of course, so long as I was back in plenty of time to face Arsenal. Holding little Mark in my arms for the first time was an amazing moment, topping anything I'd ever experienced on a football field, but I couldn't hang around for long. Anne and Mark would be down to join me in one of the club's houses in a few weeks, but, in the meantime, I had to prepare to face George Swindin's Gunners.

The 0-0 draw was the first of many matches where I saw Bert Trautmann demonstrate his immense worth to City with a string of outstanding saves. Fearless, agile and rarely out of position, Bert allowed his defenders to play with the sort of confidence that only comes when they know they can fully rely on the man behind them. Brian Clough and Peter Taylor had the right idea at Nottingham Forest when they spent an eye-watering £250,000 on Peter Shilton in 1977, reasoning that there was little point in having a first-class striker scoring goals at one end if you had a third-rate keeper letting them in at the other. Bert is rightly remembered for his heroics in the FA Cup Final, but there's no doubt that his performances in the league helped save City from relegation on more than one occasion.

By the end of October we were still unbeaten at home and were fifth in the table. There had been a couple of high-scoring blips, most notably 6-3 and 4-2 defeats at West Bromwich Albion and Everton respectively, but even these matches were closer than the results suggest. On the whole we were playing well and giving the supporters plenty to cheer about, especially when compared to the previous season. During this period we also managed to end Tottenham Hotspur's brilliant run of 11 consecutive victories with a 1-1 draw at White Hart Lane, Clive Colbridge scoring our goal. Spurs were, of course, on their way to becoming the first English team to complete the Double but, with Bert once again superb in goal, we were the first side to take a point from them during that historic season.

We enjoyed our biggest win on 29 October, beating Blackburn Rovers 4-0 at home, but the kind of blips we saw against West Brom and Everton started to become more regular – too regular for our liking. Starting against Bolton Wanderers at the beginning of November and ending against Nottingham Forest in mid-December, we went through an awful run of seven defeats in a row. This included another 6-3 reverse, this time against Chelsea and their 20-year-old goal machine, Jimmy Greaves, at Stamford Bridge. Despite still being so young, that day Jimmy clocked up his 100th league goal for the Blues on his way to one of 13 hat-tricks in only four seasons at the club. I had played with some terrific goalscorers over the last few years, but Jimmy was something else: so quick, so skilful and, ultimately, so deadly, especially inside the penalty area. It was a case of giving him an inch and him taking several miles, with the first of his goals coming after only three minutes. By the time you sniffed out the danger, Jimmy had put the ball in the back of the net again. We got off lightly compared to West Brom, however, when Jimmy scored five times in a 7-1 win a few weeks later. He scored 41 goals in only 40 league games that season before leaving for Italy and his desperately unhappy spell in Milan.

But even the emphatic scoreline doesn't tell you everything about a match in which we somehow managed to hit the woodwork four times and Denis, in particular, was always a threat. He gave us the lead after only five minutes against Aston Villa, only for us to lose 5-1. It was the first time they'd beaten us at Villa Park for more than five years and a miserable, muddy afternoon also saw me bring down Gerry Hitchens, my old Army team-mate, for a penalty to concede our third.

The terrible sequence of results saw us slip down to 14th in the table. We were still above Manchester United, but it was turning into an all-to-familiar-story for City fans as we were only four points above the relegation zone. We finally managed to stop the rot on Christmas Eve against Fulham thanks to two goals from Gerry Baker. We'd recently signed Joe's brother from a highly successful, Scottish Cup-winning spell at St Mirren, with John McTavish heading in the other direction. Although Gerry wasn't as prolific at Maine Road as he was at Love Street, he had an infectious personality and it was always nice to hear another Scottish accent in the dressing room. Gerry quipped that one of the reasons he joined City was because he'd rather be playing in a team with me than playing against me. I didn't really get that. Maybe he was getting confused between me and Dave Ewing.

For me, the only high point during our losing streak came on 9 November, when I was chosen by the Scotland selectors to play against Northern Ireland. The relief of the win over Fulham was short-lived as we lost to them at Craven Cottage two days later. This was followed by my first experience of a Manchester derby, in front of more than 60,000 supporters at

Old Trafford. We welcomed back Denis after he missed a couple of games with an ankle injury, but, just like my first experience of the Edinburgh derby, the grand occasion was one to forget. The writing was on the wall after only four minutes when Bobby Charlton put United ahead. Although Colin Barlow equalised, Alex Dawson's second hat-trick in as many matches condemned us to a 5-1 defeat – the same result I'd been on the receiving end of in my first match for Hibs against Hearts. Denis, of course, would have better days to come at Old Trafford.

Despite the challenges on the pitch, my young family and I were settling down well in Manchester. These being the days before social media and stricter dietary and health guidelines for professional footballers, I used to enjoy a few pints and – whisper it – even the odd cigar with the lads. Anne and I would also enjoy an evening out at the ballroom dancing. One of the advantages of playing for Manchester City was that the people on the door knew who I was and we didn't have to pay to get in; it was just a case of, 'Oh, hello, Jackie, in you come.' It doesn't happen so often these days. Mind you, it's been a year or two since I went ballroom dancing.

Back on the pitch, Arsenal's visit to Maine Road was considerably less one-sided than our defeat at Old Trafford, but we still didn't get the result we wanted. This time it was David Herd who scored three goals in a pulsating game that we eventually lost 5-4. Herd got a surprise when he completed his hat-trick, a young boy running on to the pitch, throwing his arms around him and kissing the bemused striker on the cheek. Luckily, the authorities took no action. It was a thrilling match and it was easy to understand people getting over-excited.

The way things were going, if Gerry or Denis had scored a hat-trick and secured us a much-needed win then I wouldn't rule out planting a smacker on them either. We were now down to 17th, an uncomfortable – but in Manchester City's case, familiar – position, and one in which a side starts to feel the dreaded suction of the relegation whirlpool.

The FA Cup provided some brief respite when we eventually managed to overcome Cardiff City at the third attempt, but we were then dumped out of the competition by Second Division Luton Town. Perhaps not surprisingly, the manager decided to make some changes. I was subsequently dropped, along with Cliff Sear, Ken Barnes and George Hannah, for the next league match against Cardiff. Dave Ewing was recalled from the reserves to play at centre-half for the first time that season and, unfortunately for me, it wouldn't be the last. I returned following the 3-3 draw at Cardiff and stayed in the side for the next seven games, during which we beat West Brom and Everton and drew with Bolton Wanderers but were beaten by Spurs, Manchester United, Blackburn, Birmingham and Preston North End.

If the Raith Rovers match was a defining moment in my career at Hibs, then our game at home to fellow relegation strugglers Preston on 31 March 1961 was my equivalent in Manchester. We hoped that we would be able to put some daylight between us and the bottom sides, especially as it was Bert's 400th league game for City, but it ended in a desperately disappointing 3-2 defeat. Once again the final result didn't tell the whole story, because it was a match we could have won had we not managed to miss two penalties. Having already seen Barrie Betts miss the target, we were presented with another chance from the spot – and with it the opportunity to rescue a draw – with five minutes to go. Under immense pressure, Joe Hayes fired our second spot-kick straight at Fred Else. Then, in a move quite out of character, Joe's frustration got the better of him and he rushed at the keeper, trying desperately to kick the ball out of his hands. Arthur Ellis, the man who had refereed Hibs' European Cup quarter-final against Djurgårdens back in 1955, then took his name. This subsequently led to fans invading the pitch and police patrolling the touchline for the last few minutes. Mr Ellis, in fairness, refused police advice to leave the stadium by the back entrance and was showered with paper, orange peel and a good deal of abuse when he left.

We were all disappointed with the result, but I, for one, could pass no judgement on our two missed opportunities. I used to practise penalties regularly in training and had taken plenty of them at school and at junior and amateur level, always managing to score. Then, when it came to taking one for Hibs' reserves at Easter Road, I got over-excited and made a crucial mistake. Anyone who has ever played golf with me has seen me do this plenty of times – I took my eye off the ball and totally skewed it. I don't think I quite managed to hit the corner flag, but it wasn't far away and it was safe to say that I wasn't put on penalty duty again.

City were now officially in trouble. We were third from bottom, level on points with Preston and only a point above Newcastle. Les decided to change things again, but, unlike the defeat to Luton Town where four of us were replaced, I was the only one left out of the team to face Wolves the following day. The manager had once again turned to his Perthshire streetfighter, Dave Ewing. The previous season, John McTavish had been playing regularly at centre-half until dropping into the Second Division had started to become a distinct possibility, so Dave was recalled with seven games to go to help City grind out the results they needed to survive. The big man had helped save the club from relegation once and, clearly, Les thought that he could do so again.

Commenting on Dave's recall in 1960-61 in the *Liverpool Echo*, Blackpool captain Jimmy Armfield said, 'Dave is a big, strong, no-nonsense type of centre-half often decried in this present age of purist soccer. But he is just what City need at the moment. There are no frills and no wanderings. When the ball gets near Dave it is instantly cleared and much of the pressure on Bert Trautmann and his colleagues is eased. It is showing in City's play and I know we are going to have tough games when we play them before the end of the season. They say it is tough at the top but, believe me, it is even tougher at the bottom.'

In a way I could understand it. Dave was clearly the kind of man who was up for a scrap, not only in his style of play but in his ability to gee up – or bawl at – his team-mates. Thankfully for Les and the Manchester City supporters, it once again paid off. Although they lost narrowly to Wolves, a run of three wins and four draws – including two against Armfield's Blackpool – was enough to secure 13th place and another season of First Division football, while Preston were relegated alongside Newcastle. I didn't feature again until the final game of the season, playing at right-half alongside Dave in a 3-3 draw at Bloomfield Road.

It was, I was convinced, going to be my last game for City because, in the wake of being dropped for the Wolves match, I had handed in a transfer request. It was almost a year to the day since I had asked for a move from Hibs, but this wasn't some twisted way of marking that unhappy anniversary. Being the only one to be left out after the Preston defeat was difficult to accept because, despite the result, I felt I had played pretty well. But even that wasn't what stung me most. It was the fact that Les made no effort to see me and explain his decision before the team left for Wolverhampton, instead leaving it to the trainer, Jimmy Meadows, to tell me that I was out.

Ian St John's relationship with Bill Shankly never recovered when he found out from Jackie Milburn that he had been dropped for a match against Newcastle at St James' Park. St John had said he was off to get changed for the match when the former Newcastle striker, by then a sports reporter, saw the team sheet and uttered the words, 'You're not playing, bonnie lad.' It was the first St John had heard of it and he was quite rightly devastated.

I'm under no illusion – there are huge differences between my situation and the Saint's. He had given more than a decade's service at Anfield while I had only been at City for a season. My team were struggling, while St John had been the heartbeat of a team that had won two league titles and an FA Cup at the beginning of a magnificent era of success. Shankly was building for the future, while Les was fighting for survival. Nevertheless, the principle was the same. It boiled down to a basic lack of respect. Don't get me wrong, I know how hard it must be for any manager to deliver bad news, but countless doctors and police officers have had to deliver far worse. We're grown men, we can take it, but the least our managers can do is tell us to our faces that we haven't made the cut. Les finally spoke to me on 6 April to tell me that, despite the threat of relegation, the Manchester City board had agreed to my request because they 'didn't want to keep an unhappy player'.

As I said at the time, City had been extremely good to me and it wasn't a case of trying to desert a club that was in trouble. If we did end up being relegated to the Second Division then I would have been happy to go with them and fight for promotion, but I could only do that if I was in the team. Nobody wanted relegation, and I wanted to continue to do my best and help my team stay up.

I understood that it was the manager's job to pick the side, but I just wanted to be shown a bit of respect, especially as I had recently helped Scotland to their first victory in over a year and I had every intention of playing for my country again.

10

Southern Discomfort

I DIDN'T stay on the transfer list at Manchester City for long. In fact, it was little over a month before I withdrew my request. I was buoyed somewhat by the fact that I was recalled for the last game of the season, albeit playing slightly out of position, but I shouldn't have got my hopes up. Dave Ewing carried on where he left off and, when he left the club, Bill Leivers took over in the middle. Although he was a centre-half when he arrived from Chesterfield in 1953, he played at right-back during the majority of his time at City. A wholehearted defender, Bill also had a tendency to get injured, which is the only reason I managed to clock up two whole appearances during the 1961/62 season: a defeat at Blackburn Rovers and a win over Aston Villa. The games took place five months apart.

While I had previously been worried about winning another Scotland cap, I was now just worried if I would ever be a first-team regular again. As an industry, football has a short memory and I felt that, the longer I was out of the limelight the more likely I was to be forgotten. I said at the time that 'at 24, I don't want to be a permanent reserve'. City had fared only slightly better in 1961/62, finishing 12th, level on points with Blackpool in 13th and only one point ahead of Leicester in 14th, so I told myself my cameo potentially made at least some small difference in the league standings.

The only advantage of being away from the pressures of first-team football was that I had more time to practise some of my party pieces. I was first shown the coin trick by Dave Mackay while on Scotland duty a year earlier. Denis Law, Alex Young and I were in the hotel lobby in Glasgow, watching in amazement as the former Hearts captain, now continuing to carve out his legend at Spurs, placed a penny on his foot and, with a deft flick into the air, he then caught it gently on his forehead before nodding it into his shirt pocket.

'How did you do that?' I asked, open-mouthed.

He just flashed me that cheeky grin of his and said, simply, 'Practice.'

So I practised, over and over, until not only could I flick a coin on to my forehead from my toe, but I could nod it back on to my foot and repeat the trick several times over. I'd always been good at keepie-ups, dating back to those early days in Holytown, when my friend Davie and I would walk from my house to the park, keeping the ball up in the air between us without once letting it touch the ground. I used to juggle the ball during my pre-match warm-ups at Maine Road, kicking it from boot, to thigh, to head, to shoulders, then back down my body to start again. It always went down well in front of the fans, but then, upstairs in the snooker room, I took it to the next level. I think you must either be pretty brave or pretty stupid to throw a billiard ball up into the air and then catch it on the back of your neck. Perhaps I was somewhere in between. Unlike taking a penalty or swinging a golf club, there was an extra incentive to keep your eye on the ball – namely, not fracturing your skull. Fortunately, I never missed but I have to reiterate the warning from Fred Eyre: don't try this at home. Or anywhere else, for that matter.

But fun as these distractions were, all I really wanted to do was play football. Following the frustrations of the 1961/62 season, the new campaign had barely begun when I was unexpectedly given another chance. After another season of flirting with relegation after selling star player Denis Law to Torino, losing 8-1 to Wolves on the opening day probably wasn't the start Les McDowall had been hoping for. Even our solitary strike at Molineux was courtesy of a Wolves player and the manager made three changes for the next match at home to newly promoted Liverpool.

After seven years away from the top flight, Bill Shankly had assembled a team that would go on to form a 'bastion of invincibility', win the First Division title at only the second attempt and ultimately dominate English and European football for the next two decades. We both secured our first point of the season with our teenage forward Neil Young cancelling out both a Ronnie Moran penalty and then an excellent strike by Roger Hunt. Just like the hugely successful Liverpool sides throughout the 1960s, 1970s and 1980s, Shankly's team contained several Scots, including big Ron Yeats and, the subject of my favourite Army taunt, Ian St John.

Of course, talented Scottish players were to be found throughout the English game at that time. On the blue side of Merseyside, for example, former Hearts striker Alex Young, known by his adoring Goodison fans as 'The Golden Vision', was helping to lead Everton to their first post-war league title; Denis Law, after his brief sojourn to Italy, was now mesmerising the crowds at Old Trafford; while Dave Mackay and John White were key members of Spurs' Double-winning side of 1961.

Another compatriot joined the City ranks for the next game when Alex Harley made his debut against Aston Villa at Maine Road. Les had shelled out the not inconsiderable sum of £20,000 on the Third Lanark striker, who in 1961 had scored a Joe Baker-equalling 42 league goals in his homeland. The visit of Aston Villa was significant for me as, with Bill Leivers out injured, it was the first time I had started back-to-back matches for the first team in nearly two and a half years. During the Liverpool game I had felt almost like an interloper at first, as though I had no business being there and there must have been some mistake on the team sheet, so it was great to be selected again, even if I was fairly certain it would be temporary.

We kept Villa at bay until the second half before Harry Burrows struck twice and the unfortunate Alex Harley missed a great opportunity from almost on the goal line. We then travelled to Liverpool and an incredible atmosphere among 46,000 fans at Anfield. St John put his side ahead after just three minutes but Peter Dobing's header meant we went in level at half-time. We should have stayed in the dressing room. I had rarely known anything like the sustained pressure we came under in the second half, with red wave after red wave pinning us back. Hunt brilliantly lobbed Bert Trautmann, which was no mean feat, for their second, and our goalkeeper was sportingly applauded by the Kop for brilliant saves from St John and from Jimmy Melia. But Bert was helpless to keep out two great shots from Alan A'Court and the 4-1 victory was hailed as 'the first great win of the new era' by the *Liverpool Echo*. They could say that again.

While clearly still able to offer so much to the team, Bert lost his place to his understudy Harry Dowd at the beginning of October. But he still stayed in the side a month longer than I did. Our 4-2 defeat to Spurs at White Hart Lane was to be my final match of 1962, but I was pleased for Alex, who opened his City account with a late consolation, and he would go on to score a further 30 goals in all competitions by the end of the season.

City played their last game of 1962 in the middle of December, by which point the UK was entering what became known as the 'Big Freeze' – the country's coldest winter for more than 200 years. By the end of December the snow in Manchester city centre was six inches deep and, like virtually every other aspect of British life for the next two months, the sporting calendar was thrown into chaos. It was a tough time for football fans with the word 'postponed' seen frequently on the fixtures lists throughout the winter. City didn't play another league match until the end of February, but, even after the snow had melted, I still found myself frozen out. Like many others I spent much of the winter months hunkered down at home, which was even livelier now that our second son, Scott, had arrived in January 1963. The little soul must have thought he'd been born in the Antarctic. What turned out to be my Manchester City swansong came shortly after being knocked out of the FA Cup by Second Division Norwich City. An injury to Barrie Betts in the defeat to Everton on 23 March 1963 led to my final appearance in a sky blue shirt.

By this point the club were fourth from bottom. Although level on points with defending champions Ipswich Town, the Big Freeze meant that we had five matches in hand. We squandered this one, however, with a 5-2 defeat at home to Burnley, who were still in the hunt for their third league title. It wasn't the worst result of the season by any means. In addition to the opening day hammering by Wolves, City had gone down 6-1 at home to West Ham back in September and been trounced 6-0 by Birmingham City, who were on their way to their first major trophy, in the quarter-finals of the League Cup.

Although they enjoyed victories over Arsenal and Spurs, successive defeats to Sheffield United, West Brom, Blackburn, Blackpool and Villa meant they needed to beat West Ham at Upton Park on the last day of the season to have any chance of staying up. Although hard to believe, the Manchester United of Matt Busby, Denis Law and Bobby Charlton were also in danger of going down to the Second Division, but a win over Leyton Orient – who were already relegated – ensured their survival. The same, unfortunately, couldn't be said of their neighbours, who, for the second time that season, lost 6-1 to the Hammers. Birmingham, the other contenders for the drop, beat Leicester and gave their fans top-flight survival to celebrate alongside their League Cup win.

After 13 years at the helm, during which he had led Manchester City to two FA Cup Finals and masterminded the 'Revie Plan', Les McDowall resigned in the wake of relegation. His assistant, George Poyser, took over on 12 July. George struggled in his quest to bring City back up, finishing sixth in his first season and 11th in his second, after which he was sacked and the hugely successful Joe Mercer era began. Among the players to pick up multiple trophies under the former Everton and Arsenal star were Alan Oakes, Neil Young, and Oakes's cousin, Glyn Pardoe. Aged only 15 when he made his debut towards the end of the 1961/62 season, some rudimentary mathematics told me that Glyn was only nine years old when I was playing in the European Cup. This was a particularly sobering thought for me, and the last thing I wanted was to begin my ninth season as a professional footballer in the reserves.

Now on the transfer list for the third time and, much to my surprise and regret, without a sniff of interest from a team in England or Scotland, I managed to persuade City to slash their asking price. Not long after I had arrived in Manchester, I said that one of the main differences between Scottish football and English football was that, in Scotland, there was a bigger gap between the top and bottom teams. Some of City's results in my final season, particularly the defeat to Wolves, clearly made a mockery of that theory. I was now going to have the chance to remind myself how big that gap in quality was in Scotland, by joining a club which – along with Hibs – had recently avoided relegation by the skin of its teeth.

By signing for Queen of the South in September 1963, I was effectively jumping from a ship that had sunk to another that was decidedly unseaworthy from the outset. After being signed by Jimmy McKinnell as a player in 1960, George Farm, the former Hibs and Scotland goalkeeper, took over as player-manager of Queens the following year. A successful playing career, during which he had spent more than a decade at Blackpool and won an FA Cup winner's medal in the 'Matthews Final' of 1953, meant George was highly respected by the players and supporters. With players like Jim Kerr and Ernie Hannigan, later of Coventry and Preston, already in Dumfries, George signed John McTurk, John Rugg, Will McLean and Neil Martin to secure promotion to the Scottish top flight during his first season in charge.

But the 1962/63 season had proved a struggle, with Queens finishing in 15th place, just a point above Hibs and three points above relegated Clyde. The club were now in an even weaker position, with Neil Martin – whose goals had been instrumental both in their promotion and in their subsequent survival – being sold to Hibs for £7,500. Jim Patterson, meanwhile, had been given a free transfer. By the time I arrived at Palmerston Park on 6 September, Queens weren't showing the kind of form that would fill their supporters with confidence.

Granted, they hadn't landed the easiest of League Cup groups, but five defeats and a draw against Rangers, Celtic and Kilmarnock, the previous season's league runners-up, suggested that another long and difficult campaign lay ahead. They had also lost their opening league fixture, 4-0 at Celtic Park, and had also been beaten by Dunfermline the day after I arrived. Not that I was in a position to do much about it, having been sent away to play with the reserves, and that's where I would stay for the next five months.

While City were prepared to let me go for £5,000, much like deals made today, they would make more money depending on the number of appearances I made for my new club and also if I was retained at the end of the season. City's assumption, like mine, was that I wasn't heading north simply as a back-up. Unfortunately, that was exactly the situation I now found myself in and it seemed there was financial pressure, right from the beginning, to limit my time in the first team.

Because the transfer from Manchester City had been arranged so quickly, my family and I had actually moved into my mother-in-law Rena's house in Holytown. She was now on her own and, because my brothers and sister were still living at home, there was no room for us at the Plenderleith inn. I did my training with Bellshill Athletic and only joined up with Queen of the South, or I should say the Queen of the South reserves, on matchdays. I didn't really get to know the manager or any of the other players particularly well, but George was a nice man and was clearly a hugely popular figure among the Palmerston support. The dangers signs were there from the start, however. The 3-1 win over Airdrie on 21 September was Queens' first victory in 19 matches. Despite wins over St Johnstone, Hearts and Hibs before Christmas, things were looking bleak, particularly when Dundee went four goals up within quarter of an hour in a 5-0 win at Palmerston. Nobody could fault George's commitment to the cause, however. After a 6-1 defeat at Partick Thistle in October, the manager took what must have been the difficult decision of dropping himself in favour of Allan Ball.

Although the young English goalkeeper, recently signed from Northern League side Stanley United, conceded six goals on his debut against Falkirk, he would go on to make more than 800 competitive appearances for the Doonhamers. But still the slide into the relegation zone continued and, three days after a

3-0 Scottish Cup defeat at home to Hearts on 25 January 1964, George was sacked – at least as manager. Despite being nearly 40 and, by his own hand, no longer being the regular pick in goal, his services as a player were retained. Queen of the South chairman Willie Harkness announced that, until a new manager was identified, the board would be selecting the team.

If they were expecting some kind of 'bounce' effect, then it backfired with the team losing their next matches 6-2 at Dundee and then 4-1 at home to Hearts. It was against this hopeless backdrop and with John Rugg having set sail for South Africa that I finally made an appearance in the Scottish First Division, four years after playing for Hibs against Raith Rovers.

Rangers, who were fighting it out with Kilmarnock for their second successive title, were the visitors. Their form was slightly better than ours having scored eight goals without reply in their last two matches, while we were second bottom of the table. Perhaps it's because it was one of the few matches I played for Queen of the South that I remember it so well. Fewer than 10,000 were there to see us take on Scot Symon's side, which included players like Jim Baxter, Willie Henderson, Ian McMillan and Jim Forrest. I had never played in a match like it. For vast swathes of the game it was really tight in the middle and not flowing anywhere – it was as though we were trying to play football in a dance hall. But McMillan played particularly well, as did Baxter, and we lost 4-1. I was given a good reception by the fans, however, and signed a few autographs – maybe I hadn't been completely forgotten after all.

I stayed in the side for the trip to Kilmarnock, where we probably deserved a point but lost 2-1 and, on 7 March, we were off to the familiar surroundings of Easter Road. As you might have gathered, I'm not really the sentimental type, but, when you're in that situation, it's difficult not to start wondering what might have been. What if I had never handed in my transfer request at Hibs? What if I hadn't gone to Manchester? Did my future lie at Easter Road after all? I didn't know, and there was little point in wasting time thinking about it. The only thing that mattered was trying to get something out of the game. We didn't get anything, and that was thanks almost entirely to the man Queens had sold to last season's relegation rivals. The Queen of the South board were now the ones left to contemplate what might have been as they watched Neil Martin score four times in Hibs' 5-2 win. It wasn't an enjoyable experience from a football point of view, but it was good to see players like Tommy Preston and John Fraser afterwards. Tommy asked me how I was doing. 'Oh, fine,' I said. There wasn't really much more I could say. My club were still without a manager, but my old team-mates were about to get a new man at the helm. The win over Queens turned out to be Walter Galbraith's final match in charge. He was replaced by Jock Stein, and it would have taken someone like the future Celtic boss to give us any chance of staying up.

Jackie Law put us in front at home to Third Lanark, the first time in 1964 that our fans had been able to watch us actually leading a match, but a Mike Jackson hat-trick condemned us to our seventh defeat in a row. That sequence was soon extended to eight as I played my last game in senior Scottish football, when we lost 3-0 to Aberdeen at Pittodrie. Dundee United then assumed the role of undertaker by hammering in the final nail of Queen of the South's First Division coffin in the next match.

A nice cup of tea is normally a good way to make you feel better following bad news, but not in our case. A faulty kettle was found to be to blame for a serious fire which broke out at Palmerston Park just three days after the loss at Tannadice, with the board room, the away dressing room and the corridor beneath the stand among the casualties. For the last two home games of the season, both teams had to get changed at the local swimming pool and travel to the ground by coach. This included the 1-1 draw with St Mirren on the last day of the season – the first point we'd managed to pick up in 13 matches.

With 23 defeats and only five victories, all five of which had come under George Farm, only East Stirlingshire had fared worse as Queen of the South said goodbye to top-flight football. In the immediate wake of Farm's sacking, Bert Houston wrote in the *Dumfries and Galloway Standard*, 'It is quite evident that Farm is being made the scapegoat for Queens' troubles. Instead of stabbing him in the back, the directors should have given him a completely free hand. After all, it was Farm who took the team from the obscurity of Second Division football into the first league. What chance had Farm had to whip the team into shape when he sees players during a game only? With the Development Club schemes and other money-raising ventures, it is about time Queens went full-time. If they don't, they will never keep their place in top league football.'

The words fell on deaf ears as, nearly half a century on, Queen of the South have yet to reappear in the top flight. George Farm, meanwhile, travelled north to Fife where he repeated what he had done in Dumfries by guiding Raith Rovers to First Division football. Like Dave Ewing when he was manager of Hibs, George would also be responsible for signing Joe Baker. After leaving Stark's Park he won the Scottish Cup with Dunfermline Athletic, before guiding them to the semi-finals of the European Cup Winners' Cup, something that not even the great Jock Stein was able to achieve with the Pars.

Following the Palmerston Park fire, chairman Willie Harkness announced, to very few people's surprise, that the club's insurance wouldn't make much of a dent in the repairs and that planned future improvements would need to be put on hold. This also meant that the chance of any full-time players being retained, particularly in the Second Division, had gone up in smoke. That suited me. After playing regularly for Hibs from just after my 17th birthday, I'd be lying if I said I thought that at the age of 26 I'd be plugging away for Queen of the South reserves. I mean absolutely no disrespect to the club, whose supporters treated me so well, but it was a bad move. People have asked me if I think I acted hastily when I handed in my transfer requests at Hibs and at Manchester City. I don't know, but what I do know is that it wasn't fair to put the blame for poor results squarely on my shoulders. The fact that City were relegated at the end of 1962/63, a season in which I played only five matches, and the fact that Hibs lost the first eight games of the season after I had left the club, is proof of that.

I'm also a firm believer in standing up for yourself and speaking out if you feel you've been treated unfairly. And, at City in particular, who was to say that, transfer request or not, I wouldn't have ended up in the reserves? That's what had happened to John McTavish after he was dropped. He eventually joined St Mirren as a makeweight in the deal to bring Gerry

Baker to Maine Road. Football really can be a cutthroat business with little to no room for sentiment.

All I knew was that, by this stage in my career, I'd more than had my fill of playing reserve-team football and, so long as I got to be first choice again, I would be prepared to go almost anywhere.

11

A New Challenge

A SEA of orange erupts as Giovanni van Bronckhorst lets fly from 30 yards and scores one of the most spectacular goals ever seen in a World Cup semi-final. The former Rangers defender's stunning strike sends the Netherlands on their way to a third appearance in the final of FIFA's global showpiece and ultimate extra-time heartache against the all-conquering Spanish.

The Netherlands are playing Uruguay in the brand-new, multimillion-pound Cape Town Stadium and South Africa has never seen anything like it. In the shadow of Table Mountain, those lucky enough to be watching the 6 July contest live are witnessing the biggest and most important football match ever played in Africa. The stories of the corruption, the bribed FIFA officials and the stolen tournament would only emerge later, but, back in the summer of 2010, hosting the FIFA World Cup was seen as an honour for the entire continent. For the Republic of South Africa, the tournament built on the success of the 1995 Rugby World Cup, when recently elected president Nelson Mandela famously donned the green jersey of the Springboks and embraced Francois Pienaar, the man mountain of a captain, as the nation truly began the healing process after more than four decades of apartheid.

As I watched the drama of the Cape Town semi-final unfold from my living room in Aberdeen, I found it hard to believe that this was the same city that my family and I had once called home. Of course a lot had happened in the world since we went to South Africa in the summer of 1964, most significantly the release of Mandela in 1990 after 27 years in prison. The intervening years had also seen me grow a lot older, a fair bit wiser and had given me plenty of time to reflect on my decision to play football in a country that practised racial segregation. It's always going to be a difficult question for me to answer and it doesn't get any easier with time.

I remember when, not long after he had been appointed England manager in 2012, Roy Hodgson's playing career came back to haunt him when a journalist asked him about his decision to join Berea Park in 1973. 'I was desperate to play professional football on a full-time basis again,' he said. 'I really didn't give the political system that much thought. It certainly played no part in my decision.'

All I can do now is offer a similar explanation. Football was still my livelihood and I had a young family to support. Had I been fully clued up – or even remotely clued up – on the politics, would I still have gone? I certainly like to think not. I'd been a professional footballer since the day I turned 17 and, while a lack of worldliness isn't an excuse, it was undoubtedly a factor. All I knew was that it had been three long years since I had last been a regular fixture in a first team line-up and it was something I missed terribly. A footballer's career is short and I felt that I had effectively lost what should have been three of the best years of my working life plugging away in the reserves. At 26, I still had a lot to give to the game that I had been playing professionally since I was little more than a boy and I also knew that I hadn't become a bad footballer overnight. That was the opinion of George Watson, Cape Town City's Scottish agent, who had contacted me early in 1964 to see if I would be interested in making the big move to Africa. I had initially turned him down, hoping that things at Queen of the South would improve or that I might be able to find another club in Scotland. It was a hell of a lot to consider. Moving to a club in England was one thing, but moving to another continent was quite another.

But the more I thought about it and discussed it with Anne, the more we came to the conclusion that we had nothing to lose. Plenty of British players had gone out to South Africa, including the great Hearts striker Alfie Conn who had joined Johannesburg Ramblers in 1960, and Queen of the South defender John Rugg who was at Durban City. And if playing for Hibs had taught me anything, it was that sometimes you had to take chances and explore new horizons. And so we decided to take a leap of faith. My mother-in-law Rena would be coming with us, which would certainly help when it came to childcare. So after saying goodbye to Queen of the South, George arranged for me to fly out to Cape Town in May.

Because the season had started in March I ended up staying and Anne, Rena, Mark and Scott, who were now aged three and one, followed on a passenger ship, the appropriately named RMS *Edinburgh Castle*, in July. I would miss my family, of course, but I was also itching to get back to playing football. I was greeted at the airport by Dirk Kemp, the Cape Town City manager. A former goalkeeper, Dirk had spent several years at Liverpool but struggled to displace fellow South African Arthur Riley before his career was interrupted by the Second World War. The fact he picked me up from the airport, took me to dinner and dropped me off at my hotel was typical of the man I would come to regard as the best manager I ever had. If you had any problems at all, professional or personal, you could talk to Dirk about it and he would go out of his way to help. I was just disappointed that I didn't get to play under him for longer.

Members of the National Football League since 1962, Cape Town City played their home games at the Hartleyvale stadium in Observatory, one of the few 'grey' suburbs in the city where all races lived together. While hardly a patch on Easter Road or Maine Road, a lot had been spent on the stadium and the team regularly drew crowds of more than 20,000. They had finished the previous season in tenth position but, with one of the best stadiums in the country, the owners were keen to have a team that matched their ambitions, as well as their infrastructure. We had some decent players, most notably the former Charlton goalkeeper Albert Uytenbogaardt, but, in the early 1970s they added a string of famous names to their ranks. These included Peter Lorimer, George Eastham, Mick Channon, Ian St John, Jim Forrest and even Geoff Hurst.

It was a beautiful country but one of the first things I had to get used to was the climate and the fact the summer months back home were the winter months in South Africa. Not that it made much difference in Cape Town where, even in the winter, I found myself taking salt tablets to help me cope with the heat and stop my muscles from seizing up. For a Lanarkshire lad who had recently been through the Big Freeze and who once had to play with bandages round his boots to stay upright on an ice-covered pitch at Easter Road, it was a bit of a shock to the system.

And while the sunshine was good for taking the kids to the beach and for playing a few rounds of golf, it could make some of the pitches like concrete. Some clubs compensated by growing longer grass, but, either way, I had to move from screw-in studs to the smaller, metal variety. They were a bit like golf shoes and much more comfortable. In terms of the quality of the football, it was probably the equivalent of the second tier in Scotland – not great, but fast and competitive. It also took me a little while to get used to the standard – or, to be kind I'll say tolerance levels – of the officials. I'd always thought of myself as a fair player, but I wasn't in my new home long before my name – or at least somebody's name – went into the book. I slid in for a tackle, the kind I'd made hundreds of times on British pitches without a word of protest, and won the ball, only to hear the referee blasting away like a whistle-happy policeman in an Ealing crime caper.

'You nearly broke his leg,' he exclaimed.

'But I got the ball!'

'You're going in the book. What's your name?'

I shrugged and said, 'Stanley Matthews.'

Although I was a long way from home, it didn't always feel like it. At one point during that first season I was one of five Scots in City's starting line-up, which also included Ian Goodall, Tommy Hannam, John Livingstone and Robert

Kerr, none of whom had exactly set the football world alight back home but were good, solid players. At the end of an unspectacular 1964 season, Dirk decided to call it a day. He was extremely popular among the players, so we were sorry to see him go. We took him out for some drinks, trying to get him to change his mind, but he told us that he'd just had enough. I wondered if Dirk's friendliness was his undoing and the owners felt that, if the team were to be successful, they would need a manager with more of a cut-throat attitude. In Reg Smith, they certainly got one.

An outside-left who was capped twice for England while at Second Division Millwall, Smith's playing career – like Dirk's – was put on hold during the war. He turned out for Dundee as a guest while stationed at RAF Leuchars in Fife and, at the end of the conflict, he joined the club for the remainder of his playing career before moving into management with Corby Town. He then joined Dundee as a coach before being poached in 1954 by city rivals Dundee United. After a couple of mid-table finishes he left Tannadice in January 1957 to join bottom-of-the-table Falkirk, where he wrote himself into Bairns folklore, not only by saving them from relegation but by guiding them to only their second – and to date last – victory in the Scottish Cup. A two-year spell at his old club Millwall followed before he was tempted out to South Africa with Addington. It was immediately following a second, unsuccessful spell at the Durban-based club – actually, while he was about to get on a plane to return to England – that he got the call to take over at Cape Town City. As far as I was concerned, it was a call I wished Reg had never answered.

The son of a South Africa rugby union international, the Londoner was a man I just didn't see eye-to-eye with. Dirk had appointed me captain and although I retained that position, Reg shifted me to full-back for the first time in my career. In one training session he was talking tactics and said, 'I want the full-backs to attack down the wing.' I just piped up and said, 'And what's the winger supposed to be doing?' He didn't answer. Man-management wasn't Reg's strongpoint, but we got results and finished the 1965 season as runners-up to Highlands Park. The Johannesburg team, who would later recruit Spurs and Dundee legend Alan Gilzean, had also captured the Castle Cup. They were a strong side and this was their fourth title in six years, but we did manage to get the better of them in the UTC Bowl.

On a memorable night in front of 23,000 – a Hartleyvale record – we knocked Highlands Park out in the first round thanks to a penalty three minutes from time. Emotions were running high and it wasn't the only controversial moment of the match. Midway through the second half I was involved in an incident with Willie McIntosh, which culminated in the outside-left kicking me in the face. I don't know whether he meant it, but it certainly left a mark and, as bottles rained on to the field from a section of the visiting supporters, the former Aberdeen player was sent off. There weren't many handshakes at the end of the match, but we were pleased to overcome the strong favourites. We went on to beat Reg Smith's former side Addington in the semi-finals before losing to Durban City in the final.

Reg and I still struggled to get on and it was probably a relief when he found an excuse to get rid of me early in the 1966 season, when I broke my arm in an awkward landing after going up for a header. I would have been happy to stay at Cape Town, despite Reg, but I was transferred to struggling Bloemfontein City for the remainder of the season. Bloemfontein was an 11-hour flight from Cape Town and, because I suspected it wouldn't be a long-term move, I rented a flat and travelled back to see my family as often as I could. Fortunately, I was able to transfer to another club in Cape Town before the season was out.

Founded by Greek South Africans in 1958, Hellenic were known as 'The Greek Gods', although it was going to take some divine intervention to turn us into champions. We had a decent seventh-placed finish in my second – and ultimately last – season in South Africa, but by then I'd had enough.

I have mixed feelings when I look back on my time in the southern hemisphere. I was only a footballer and even now, I would never be so arrogant as to believe that me taking a stand and refusing to go would have made much difference. It certainly wouldn't have made the kind of impact that multi-millionaire performers like Frank Sinatra, Elton John and Queen could have made had they turned down gigs at Sun City in the middle of a United Nations boycott. And who can forget the infamous rebel cricket tours of the 1980s and early 1990s, which included England stars like Graham Gooch, Mike Gatting and the ironically named Geoffrey Boycott?

Thankfully, the world is now a different place. The National Football League that I competed in folded in 1977 and was superseded by a non-racial league. And while I have regrets, going to South Africa at least gave me an incredible opportunity that few footballers can claim to have enjoyed.

Me at Holytown Primary School. I'm in the back row, third from the right.

With my best friend, Davie French (right), and his brother Alistair (left)

A day trip aged about 15 with mum and dad, brothers Robert and Richard and sister Anne

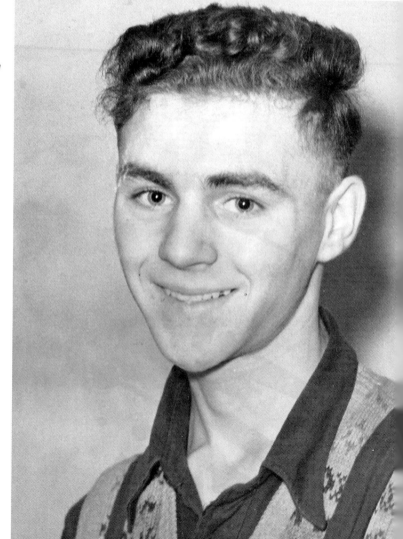

Nearly 17 and just about to sign for Hibs.
Picture: DC Thomson

A proud moment – captaining Scotland Schoolboys against Northern Ireland in Belfast, 1952. Goalkeeper Adam Blacklaw, later a title winner with Burnley, is immediately behind me in the middle row.

Showing my sister Anne how to juggle the ball in our back garden in Holytown.
Picture: DC Thomson

*Heading clear for Hibs
against Airdrie.*

Picture: The Scotsman
Publications and used with
their kind permission.

Keeping a close watch on Hibs goalkeeper Tommy Younger as he tries to gather the ball against Celtic. Picture: The Scotsman Publications and used with their kind permission.

Receiving treatment from trainer Jimmy McColl, who was a legendary player with Celtic and Hibs. Picture: The Scotsman Publications and used with their kind permission.

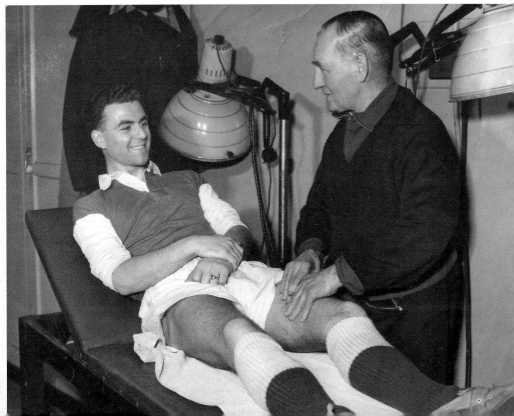

Captaining the British Army side against Hearts at Tynecastle in 1959. Picture: The Scotsman Publications and used with their kind permission.

Manchester City, 1960. Back (left to right): Me, Barrie Betts, Bert Trautmann, Ken Barnes, Cliff Sear, David Shawcross. Front: Gerry Baker, George Hannah, Denis Law, Clive Colbridge, Joe Hayes.

Ferenc Puskás, who I played against twice in two days, scores his fourth goal against Eintracht Frankfurt in the 1960 European Cup Final at Hampden Park.

With my sons Mark, left, and Scott at Mark's wedding in Australia.

On the way to watch Hibs take on Rot-Weiss Essen on the 50th anniversary of our first European Cup match with, from left to right, Tommy Preston, Lawrie Reilly and Jimmy 'Tiger' Thomson.

12

Puskás

SOME FOOTBALLERS are lucky if they come up against a player of Ferenc Puskás's calibre once in a lifetime, so whatever wrong turns I might have taken during my career I must have done something right to have come up against the legendary Hungarian twice in the space of two days.

The great man himself must have thought the same, doing a double-take and then signalling to one of his Real Madrid team-mates when he realised that the player standing across from him in the Cape Town tunnel was indeed the same Jackie Plenderleith he had played against in Johannesburg the previous evening. It's no wonder he was surprised to see me again, with around 800 miles and a two-hour flight separating the two cities. But then the superstars of Real Madrid, including 'Galacticos' such as Puskás, and Spanish internationals Paco Gento and Amancio Amaro, were being handsomely rewarded for their 1964 tour of South Africa, where they would play two exhibition matches in front of capacity crowds.

It's probably a safe bet that Hungary's 'Galloping Major' pocketed more money than I did for those two appearances, but here I was, popping up again like a bad penny. Not that I minded. For younger readers it's hard to overstate just what a colossus Puskás was, and I'm not referring to his robust frame. His former international team-mate Zoltán Czibor probably summed up Puskás best when he said, 'If he kicked the ball once, he scored two goals.' It wasn't much of an exaggeration. Even today, Puskás lies third on the list of all-time international goalscorers with his 84 strikes for Hungary coming in only 85 games and, in total, he scored more than 800 goals throughout his career. He was the man who helped his country to a gold medal at the 1952 Olympic Games and so nearly led the Magnificent Magyars to World Cup glory against West Germany in 1954, scoring Hungary's second in a surprise 3-2 defeat in the final. He had earlier been England's tormentor in chief when trouncing them 6-3 at Wembley and then 7-1 in Budapest, two results which proved definitively that the birthplace of football had been left in the wake of some of its international rivals.

But it was in the famous all-white strip of Real Madrid that Puskás – as much as anybody – was responsible for ensuring the continued popularity of the European Cup. And there was one match in particular that secured his legacy in Real's colours. In front of nearly 130,000 spectators at Hampden Park, Puskás scored four goals in Real's stunning 7-3 victory over Eintracht Frankfurt in the 1960 European Cup Final. In doing so, he managed to outdo even the legendary Alfrédo Di Stefano, who scored the other three. Probably the greatest match ever played on Scottish soil and one of the best games in history saw Real secure their fifth successive title and ensured that European club competition was here to stay.

As footballing achievements go, any comparisons between Puskás and myself probably begin and end with us both having competed in the European Cup. I can, however, claim the bragging rights of appearing in the tournament before he did, with his previous club Honvéd turning down the invitation to take part in 1955. Even in defeat Puskás was magnificent, which he proved when he racked up another hat-trick in the 1962 final, this time in a 5-3 loss to Benfica. There wasn't a footballer alive who wouldn't have relished the chance to play against Puskás, even if – by 1964 – the 37-year-old's career was apparently winding down.

Just ask Fred Eyre, who was an apprentice while I was at Manchester City. In his bestselling book, *Kicked Into Touch*, which details his struggles as a reserve-team footballer, Fred recalls the time he provided an 'assist' for Puskás when he spotted him taking a training session in Australia. He described being able to pass the ball to the then 64-year-old as 'the stuff of dreams'. It's no wonder that FIFA named its annual competition for the world's greatest goal in Puskás's honour. Lining up against him, even in an exhibition match, was quite a step up from Fred's experience, but I'd be lying if I said I imagined that I'd be playing for a pub team. That's not true, of course, but my first match against Real Madrid was in the colours of a 'Lager XI'.

Bringing the world's most famous football team down from Spain wasn't going to be cheap and South African Breweries – owners of Castle Lager and sponsors of South Africa's equivalent of the FA Cup – stepped in to meet the shortfall. So the 'Castle Knights' were born and, despite the odds being stacked against us, we were all well up for our jousting match with the kings of European football. Yes, it was a friendly, but try telling that to the 35,000 spectators who spent their hard-earned rand to see Puskás and company in the flesh. No member of the Castle Knights squad was under any illusion about which team the fans were there to see. I remember hearing a story about the time Hibs played Barcelona at Murrayfield in 2008. My old club had knocked the Catalans out of the Inter-Cities Fairs Cup with an amazing 7-6 aggregate win back in 1961, but it was fair to say that something of a gulf had developed in the intervening years. Barcelona fielded a full-strength side in Edinburgh, including Thierry Henry, Eidur Gudjohnsen and a rising young superstar named Lionel Messi.

When the inevitable happened and Hibs found themselves 3-0 down after only 18 minutes, one supporter grabbed his six-year-old son by the hand and marched him out of the stadium in disgust. I don't really know what he was expecting, but you can be sure that barely a day goes by that his now teenage son doesn't remind him of the day he dragged him away from a rare opportunity to watch some of the world's greatest players in the flesh. These are times when you want to say, 'I was there.' Not, 'I was there for a few minutes before my dad took the huff.' Players like Messi are the kind that many people will be lucky to get to see once in a lifetime, so, whatever the score, you should try to enjoy every minute of the experience.

That said, there was still pride at stake among the Castle Knights and our manager. The man chosen to select the South Africa XI was experienced in football as well as life. Originally from Glasgow, Jimmy Clark was no stranger to success having won the First Division title as a centre-half with Sunderland in 1935/36. A man of meticulous planning, Jimmy was a bomber pilot during the Second World War. He was also a football fanatic and owned a library of books, periodicals and newspapers on the subject. When the former Cape Town City manager, who had led Southern Suburbs to victory in the Bowl the previous season, was given the job of selecting a South African XI to face Real Madrid, he immediately set to work.

One magazine in his collection contained a large, in-depth feature devoted to Real Madrid's recent European Cup Final defeat to Inter Milan. It was written in Italian, so Jimmy visited some Italian football fans in Durban to have the articles translated. He also read up as much as he could about Real and watched and then re-watched the television footage of their famous win over Eintracht Frankfurt. Nobody could accuse Jimmy of being underprepared. At the same time, everyone knew that the main objective, from a South African point of view, was to keep the score down to a respectable level.

Choosing who would face touring sides – which in recent years had included Leicester City, Arsenal and Spurs – had previously been done by committee. These selection committees, however, had been accused of pandering to supporters, making sure there were plenty of local players for fans to cheer on in cities like Durban and Johannesburg. Jimmy, who had been given sole responsibility of selecting the Castle Knights, didn't care. He knew the fans were there to see Real Madrid and that it was his job to give them as competitive a game as possible. I like to think Jimmy thought I would bring a bit of flair to the side. Watching me go through one of my ball-juggling routines in training, he told a journalist, 'Look at him – a half-back as good with the ball as most top-class forwards.' I would also have to be on my game in defence – just standing in the middle of the park doing keepie-ups wouldn't do me much good against some of the world's greatest footballers.

To the chagrin of some, Jimmy's 14-man squad contained a total of eight players from overseas, all whom were relatively new to South African football. As well as me, the squad included Keith Blackburn, who had signed for Durban City from Portsmouth, David Pygall, formerly of Watford and now of Highlands Park, and John Rugg, the centre-half whose transfer to Durban meant I finally managed to get some game time with Queen of the South. We had some decent local talent in the side too, including midfielder Freddie Kalk of Highlands Park, the most expensive player in the National Football League, and Les Salton, the Durban United forward who had more than 200 goals to his name. Our most dangerous weapon came in the form of Bobby Chalmers. The 23-year-old Rhodesian had been banging in goals all season, including six in a Castle Cup tie against Port Elizabeth City.

Jimmy had chosen Rugg to captain the side, so it was no surprise that I found myself at right-back, but I was just very excited at the thought of playing against Real Madrid, a team I had admired for years but had long since given up hope of ever playing against. I might have had the chance to face them in the European Cup Final had Hibs managed to overcome Reims a few years earlier, but that was as close as I'd got. It didn't bother me that this would be a friendly either. After all, this type of fixture had allowed me to come up against some of the all-time greats, including John Charles and Tom Finney, while at Hibs. Not long after I arrived in South Africa in May 1964, I had represented Western Province against Arsenal in Cape Town. The following month, I played for a Free State Invitational XI in Bloemfontein against Eintracht Frankfurt, the team Puskás had so tormented at Hampden. These matches were great to be part of, but there was the sense among every one of the Castle Knights that playing against Miguel Muñoz's Real Madrid was going to be something special. I was never one to be starstruck, but the thought of sharing a pitch with Puskás made me feel like a kid in a toy shop.

Not everyone understood what it meant, however. The match described by the *Rand Daily Mail* as 'South Africa's greatest soccer showpiece ever' was accompanied by quite possibly the world's most boring souvenir programme. A front cover which should have featured a picture of some of the great Real players in action instead showed a bunch of officials in suits signing the agreement that brought the Spanish team to South Africa. I know we tend to go the other way in terms of hype these days, but I'm sure the marketing team could have done better than this.

Not that it kept the crowds away with the Rand Stadium, which was then home to Highlands Park, packed to the rafters for the Tuesday evening kick-off in Johannesburg. And I can't imagine it was cheap to get in either, with the cost of putting on the contest thought to be in the region of £600,000 in today's money. The organisers had certainly rolled out the red carpet for our illustrious visitors, with parades and marching bands helping to whip the crowd up into a frenzy.

In terms of looking after himself, Puskás wasn't Cristiano Ronaldo, another Real Madrid legend and one of the few players worthy of the great man's mantle. But then, even in his pomp, the Hungarian had never been considered svelte. With his vision, touch, power and skill, however, he didn't need to be. Walking out of the Wembley tunnel ahead of Hungary's famous victory in 1953, Billy Wright dismissed the Olympic champions' chances based on the fact that they 'hadn't got the proper kit'. That was before Puskás had left the England captain on his backside with a sublime drag-back and then fired the ball past Gil Merrick with that incredible left foot of his. His right foot really was just for standing on.

Wright's wayward attempt at a sliding tackle was memorably described by Geoffrey Green in *The Times* as being 'like a fire engine going to the wrong fire'. Even at 37, Puskás's remarkable talent was still burning bright and, although the match wasn't competitive, I didn't want to be similarly labeled as a misguided appliance. As a team I think we did ourselves proud, particularly with the frighteningly quick Gento, one of Spain's all-time greats, causing us no end of problems down the left wing. We also had to contend with Lucien Muller, the France international right-half who had signed from Reims, while John Rugg's opposite number was José Santamaría, who had clocked up nearly 40 international appearances between his native Uruguay and Spain.

When the game began I was initially confused because I kept hearing a short, shrill whistle above the roar of the crowd. At first I assumed it was the referee, but then I realised that it was actually coming from Puskás. Every time he wanted the ball he'd emit this piercing whistle, like a contestant on *One Man and His Galactico*. He'd receive the ball then play another inch-perfect pass for yet another attack. He was clearly pacing himself in Johannesburg's high altitude but he was still deadly. Our resistance didn't last long with Gento, the captain, beating our goalkeeper Trevor Gething with a powerful shot from outside the box after only five minutes. Real then stepped up a gear and, after hitting the woodwork a couple of times, Félix Ruiz and then Puskás added to the Spaniards' tally with long-range shots of their own. We were 3-0 down at half-time but, no matter where their allegiances lay, nobody was leaving the stadium.

And it was a good thing, too. Real made three changes at half-time but, perhaps surprisingly, veteran Puskás wasn't among them. We pushed them back at the beginning of the second half and Bobby Chalmers, completely unfazed by the occasion, pulled a goal back. Our great comeback didn't last long, however, when Amancio Amaro made it 4-1. Many, including me, felt that Puskás was offside, but he was Ferenc Puskás – he could do what he liked. Like the great Hungarian, Amancio would end up with a glowing footballing CV. Nicknamed 'El Brujo' (The Magician), the outside-right had helped Spain win their first European Championship title a couple of months earlier. He later scored the opening goal in Real's 2-1 win over Partizan Belgrade in the 1966 European Cup Final and won a total of nine La Liga titles at the Bernabéu. Amancio struck again to make it 5-1 and then, with five minutes to go, Chalmers completed a memorable evening with his second. Scoring a brace against one of the world's greatest teams certainly did Bobby's confidence no harm and he would go on to become the highest scorer in the history of the National Football League. I was pleased with how I'd performed, with the *Cape Argus* describing me as the Knights' 'outstanding player'. Maybe I would have fared quite well against Raymond Kopa back in 1955 after all.

As both sets of players were applauded from the pitch, I joked to John Rugg that I would make sure I avenged our defeat the following evening. I was the only player who would be lucky enough to repeat the experience in Cape Town, so I made sure I went straight to bed when I returned to the hotel to catch my morning flight.

The next day, I was back on home turf at Hartleyvale when I spotted a familiar face in goal. Jackie Wren, the keeper I'd played alongside at Hibs before going to Manchester City, was now at Hellenic and, like me, had been selected for a Western Province XI to face Real. After turning out for Rotherham, Stirling Albion and Berwick Rangers, Jackie had gone to South Africa at the same time as me. It was the first time I'd seen him since 1960.

'Hi Jackie,' I said. 'Do you remember the last time we played together?'

He smiled and said, 'Of course, Jackie, how could I forget? It was a Scottish Cup tie against Hearts – you scored an own goal, I conceded five and we both got dropped!'

In the end we fared better against Real Madrid, if only slightly, than we did against Hearts. Jackie played pretty well in goal and I enjoyed being back in my favoured position at centre-half but neither of us was able to stop the Spanish onslaught. Once again Gento and Puskás were outstanding up front, sharing all the goals in a 4-0 win. We could have done with the in-form Chalmers up front, but it was unlikely to have made a great deal of difference. Gento was probably the fastest footballer I ever faced, with the Spaniard likely to give one of South Africa's cheetahs a run for its money. He won a record six European Cups during his 18 years at Madrid, and it was easy to see why. Although it was a friendly, he made scoring a hat-trick look easy, while he also supplied a sublime cross for Puskás to bullet a header past Jackie for Real's second. Having faced them myself, I was particularly impressed when my old friends at Hibs beat Real 2-0 at Easter Road just a few weeks later, with 19-year-old local lad Peter Cormack opening the scoring.

I wasn't on the winning side in Johannesburg or in Cape Town but never after such heavy back-to-back defeats had I ever felt so satisfied. Even after two losses in two days, it had been an incredible experience and undoubtedly the highlight of my four years in South Africa. Coming up against Gento and his team-mates was special, but the moment when Puskás nodded his head towards me in the Cape Town tunnel, as though to say 'we meet again' is something that – like Fred Eyre's encounter with the great man in Australia – I'll never forget.

Even a year later, at the grand old age of 38, Puskás could still be prolific. After winning his fifth La Liga title with Real, he played a part in their sixth European Cup victory, scoring four goals in 20 minutes during a 5-0 win over Feyenoord in the preliminary round. Although I didn't manage to swap shirts with him in either match, I was to get hold of Santamaría's. And while many of my prized football possessions I accumulated managed to disappear into the ether over the years, I at least managed to find out what became of it.

In between moves back home, I'd left the shirt at my parents' house. Many years later I was having dinner with them and I asked my dad if he knew where Santamaría's shirt was. He finished a mouthful of mince and tatties and looked at me sheepishly before leading me through to his bedroom, where he proceeded to pull a now-black shirt out of his chest of drawers. It turned out he'd been wearing it down the coal mine and the famous white kit was now unrecognisable. I laughed and said, 'Well, Dad, bang goes my last chance to wear a Real Madrid shirt!'

But while I never got to don a white jersey, I did have the privilege of wearing a dark blue one.

13

A Dream Come True

MY SON Scott has never forgiven me for choosing to join Manchester City.

It's not because he's a United fan, just a dyed-in-the-wool Scotsman and, because I was playing at Maine Road when he was born in January 1963, for almost 60 years he's had to suffer the 'torment' of having an English birthplace on his passport. I've occasionally wound him up about it, asking why an Englishman like him gets upset when Scotland lose, something that's happened far more often than we would like over the years. But Scott, like his older brother Mark, is very proud of the fact his father played for his country, even if it was only once at senior level.

I think it's because it was a solitary appearance that it means so much to me. Long after winning two European Cups as manager of Nottingham Forest, Brian Clough cited his two appearances for England as among his proudest achievements. I didn't have the same kind of medal collection as Clough, so I think my lone cap shines even brighter. It certainly seemed to take a long time in coming. I'd been touted as a possible successor to George Young – the first man to clock up 50 appearances for Scotland – since I was a teenager at Hibs. And though I had to wait until I was a 23-year-old at Manchester City, I couldn't have been more excited or proud when the big call finally came. Had I been playing in another era, the call would never have come at all. There was a period in the late 19th century when the Scottish Football Association refused to consider selecting 'Anglos' – Scots plying their trade for English clubs. Had this short-sighted policy still been in place in November 1960 I'd have missed out on my cap, and Scotland would also have had to do without the services of Tottenham's Dave Mackay, as well as my City team-mate Denis Law.

Although this was to be the first time I had represented Scotland at the highest level, I had first pulled on international colours back in May 1952 when I had the honour of captaining the Scotland Schoolboys Under-14s against Northern Ireland. I had attracted the attention of the selectors with good performances for Lanarkshire Schools against a Glasgow select, which we won 2-0, and also for a West of Scotland versus East of Scotland schools match.

The game against Northern Ireland in Belfast was especially memorable for me as it was my first trip 'overseas', and we even enjoyed a stroll on Bangor beach beforehand. My young international career got off to a great start as we won 5-2 at Grosvenor Park, which was then the home ground of Distillery. As is often the case with schoolboy football, not everyone goes on to make the grade as a professional. Indeed, not all of them want to, especially in an era when being a top footballer would earn you no more money than a being a tradesman. But among the boys I played with that day in Belfast were inside-right Billy Reid, who spent six years at Motherwell before joining Airdrie, and goalkeeper Adam Blacklaw. After joining Burnley straight from school as an apprentice, the Aberdonian found lasting fame with the Clarets as part of their First Division championship side of 1960. He also picked up an FA Cup runners-up medal in 1962 as well as three full caps for Scotland.

I continued to make good progress and, while at Ferndale Athletic, the Scottish Junior FA called me up to play for the Under-18s. It was February 1953, less than a year after I had played for the Under-14s and only four months after my 15th birthday. This time, I would be playing all three of the other Home Nations in the Schoolboy Championship, with England first up at Ibrox. For a young Rangers supporter, the thought of walking out on to the Govan turf was an exciting enough prospect, but to be doing it while wearing the Lion Rampant on my chest was an incredibly proud moment. All that stuff about the 'Auld Enemy' has been said plenty of times, but there was no doubt they were the team we really wanted to beat. And, when we raced into a 3-0 lead in Glasgow, it looked like that's what we were going to do, only for England to fight back and beat us 4-3. That was a hard one to take, both for the young players and for Thomas Kerr, the Lord Provost of Glasgow, who was watching from the stands.

I returned to Belfast, this time to the Oval, for a 1-1 draw with Northern Ireland before I made my first visit to Tynecastle for a hard-fought game against Wales. That goalless draw was my last international involvement for nearly three years, when I was called up by the Scotland Second XI Association to play in two trial matches for the Under-23s. It was December 1955 and, by this time, I had been in the Hibs first team for more than a year. We had recently beaten Djurgårdens to reach the semi-finals of the European Cup and the trial matches also had an exciting prize on offer – they would help determine who would be picked to play against England's Under-23s on 8 February. Playing alongside my Hibs team-mate Tommy Preston, we enjoyed a 5-1 win over Clyde. But while we impressed in the pouring rain at Shawfield, we would have to contend with far worse conditions in our next game, which would be against very familiar opponents.

With the obvious exceptions of Tommy and myself, Hibs fielded a full-strength side for the trial match in January 1956, but I still find it incredible to think that it went ahead. After deeming the frozen Easter Road surface playable, it wouldn't have surprised me if the officials had gone to Murrayfield Ice Rink and thought that was also ideal for a game of football. I had tried to play on ice when I was a boy and didn't know any better, but we were supposed to be professionals. The idea behind the trial matches was that we would be properly tested, but it seemed like an unnecessary risk for the teams involved, especially on a pitch like that.

After going out to take a look at the surface beforehand and realising that it didn't give a centimetre beneath our studs, a few of us exchanged worried glances and decided to take action. We didn't do anything drastic, we just grabbed some bandages from the trainer's bag and wrapped them round our boots in the hope it would give us some much-needed traction. But it turned out the person who really needed bandages was Willie Ormond. It had taken only five minutes for the inevitable to happen. Willie went down in a tackle with Falkirk's Alex Parker – later of Everton – and then had to be led from the field and straight to the Western General Hospital with a fractured wrist. Much to Hugh Shaw's annoyance, he was out for four matches.

The surface was so slippery that if you missed the ball, you couldn't just stop and immediately change direction. Instead you were forced, as Gair Henderson put it so wonderfully in the *Evening Times*, 'to circle like an aircraft round a landing field before coming in for a second attempt'. Hearts' Willie Duff, our goalkeeper, was wearing trousers and you could almost hear the sharp intakes of breath among the 20,000 crowd any time he and opposite number Tommy Younger dived on the ground. Both were black and blue afterwards. Eddie Turnbull, a man who wouldn't have batted an eyelid had he been asked to play on solid concrete, scored a hat-trick, while John Frye, who had bravely stepped on in place of Willie Ormond, also scored. Rangers' Alex Scott got one for the Under-23s and, despite the defeat, Tommy and I did enough to impress the selectors. We were both thrilled to be chosen to play at Hillsborough where we looked forward to pitting ourselves against England's left-half – a highly rated teenager named Duncan Edwards.

Earning your first cap for the 'Colts' was an important milestone. Unlike so many Under-21 players of recent years, who subsequently never got so much as a sniff of a full cap, the Under-23 sides were a far more integral part of the international set-up. Edwards, for example, already had four caps for England by the time the match in Sheffield came around, while Denis

Law made his Scotland debut as an 18-year-old before playing a game at Under-23 level.

The good news of my own selection had come hot on the heels of our 7-0 win over Motherwell in the league and, after learning that I would be playing against England, I had an extra spring in my step for that weekend's Scottish Cup tie against Raith Rovers. I don't know whether lessons had been learned from Willie Ormond's injury a few weeks earlier, but bad weather forced the postponement of the match to the following Wednesday – the day Tommy and I were meant to be travelling down to Sheffield. The day beforehand, Hibs announced that they were withdrawing us from the team to face England with our team-mate Bobby Nicol taking my place and Falkirk's Jimmy McIntosh being called up to replace Tommy. I don't know if my performances suffered as a result of having my first Under-23 cap snatched from my grasp by bad weather, but it probably didn't help and I was dropped by Hibs shortly afterwards.

Tommy and I weren't the only ones to miss out on the game as a result of cup duty, with Chelsea withdrawing Frank Blunstone and Peter Sillett, so they could play against Burnley in an FA Cup replay on the Monday. Scotland ended up losing 3-1 but I would love to have played. It was an early taste of the disappointment of missing out against England at international level, and it wouldn't be the last.

While upset at being withdrawn at the last minute, I could at least understand Hibs' decision and it showed that – at least for the time being – they saw me as a valuable member of the team. I was given another opportunity to play for the Under-23s a year later but, for some clubs, the risk of allowing their players to appear in trial matches was simply too great. Partick Thistle, for example, refused to allow Tommy Ewing to play against Rangers in January 1957, and he subsequently wasn't considered for the team to play England the following month. Tommy did, however, win the first of two full caps later in the year against Wales.

By this time I was back in the Hibs team and, on a heavy pitch in front of a crowd of 15,000, me and the other Under-23 trialists – including Dave Mackay of Hearts – managed to grind out a 3-3 draw at Ibrox. I was subsequently chosen to earn my first Under-23 cap against England at the same ground on 26 February and – with Hibs having already been knocked out of the Scottish Cup by Aberdeen – not even the wildest of wild horses would be able to keep me away. The fact that my first cap would come a year later than expected made the experience all the sweeter. I wasn't the only Under-23 player making my debut at Ibrox, with Hearts winger Ian Crawford and St Mirren goalkeeper Campbell Forsyth also making their first appearance at this level. England, meanwhile, handed debuts to Jack Dyson, who had scored in Manchester City's FA Cup win over Birmingham City the previous season, and to Brian Clough of Middlesbrough.

Duncan Edwards, unfortunately, wouldn't be playing but England still boasted several excellent players. In addition to Clough, they also fielded future England captains Johnny Haynes and Ronnie Clayton, who between them would go on to clock up more than 90 appearances at senior level, while my opposite number Trevor Smith is still held in legendary regard by Birmingham fans. England also had an extremely talented

21-year-old outside-left in the form of Manchester United's David Pegg. Like Edwards, Pegg would be dead less than a year later, killed on the icy runway at Munich.

England were a good side, but, starting with Dave Mackay, we had some decent players of our own, including our skipper's team-mates Alex Young and Ian Crawford, and Rangers full-back Eric Caldow, who would go on to win 40 caps for Scotland, 15 of them as captain.

There was an eerie atmosphere in what was only the third Under-23 international between the countries as a layer of fog drifted in from the Clyde and the cheers of the 30,000 crowd became intertwined with the sound of ships' foghorns. The sight of these ghost-like figures in white, who to me seemed about ten feet tall emerging from the mist, was like something out of the video game *Silent Hill* – apparently.

It took only 12 minutes for our apparition-like opponents to take the lead through Dyson, who brought down Pegg's cross with his right foot before burying it high past Campbell Forsyth with his left. Our goalkeeper, then with St Mirren, would win four caps for Scotland while with Kilmarnock and kept a clean sheet in his first match against England in April 1964. This was significant as, along with Alan Gilzean's header, it helped complete Scotland's hat-trick over England – their only three-game winning streak against their neighbours in the 20th century.

Dyson, the man who beat Campbell on his only Under-23 appearance, played first-class cricket for Lancashire after hanging up his football boots, but we had no intention of skulking back to the pavilion. England, especially Haynes, probably had the greater skill, but we were up for the fight. Mackay, in particular, was really getting stuck in and we were lucky not to concede a penalty when he brought down Lincoln City's Richard Neal in the box. We were awarded a spot-kick of our own just before the half-hour when Neal brought down Alex Young. His team-mate Ian Crawford, on his only appearance for Scotland at any level, fired past Sheffield United's Alan Hodgkinson for the equaliser.

Ian was a perfect example of why it sometimes pays to persevere in football. The outside-left started out at Easter Road as a youngster but, thanks to the Famous Five, was unable to break into the first team. After a spell at Hamilton he ended up at Hearts. He won two league championships and scored twice in the 1956 Scottish Cup Final win over Celtic before later playing alongside Bobby Moore at West Ham United. If he'd penned an autobiography in the style of Alan Partridge, this is the point where he'd be writing, 'Needless to say, I had the last laugh.'

Ian's goal secured a 1-1 draw but I was particularly pleased with the match report in the *Glasgow Herald*, which said, 'Scotland had no better player than Plenderleith, who by skilful methods alone mastered the taller, heavier Clough, whose name is pronounced as in rough and who later admitted the young Hibernian centre-half's superiority by acting somewhat rough. Perhaps he was irritated too by his failure to score at least three goals early in the match and at least one in the second half.'

I picked up my second Under-23 cap in the team's next appearance later in the year, when Dave Mackay led us to a 4-1 win over the Netherlands at Tynecastle. It was only the second time that Scotland had faced the Dutch at international level with Dave, a regular penalty taker for Hearts and easily our best player on the night, burying our fourth goal from the spot to maintain our country's 100 per cent record. My call-up came at just the right time as, when the game was played on 23 October, I had lost my place in the Hibs line-up to Jock Paterson. One report said I looked short of match practice, but that was nothing compared to my third Under-23 cap – my second appearance against England. I think I was as surprised as anyone to find myself in the team for the game at Goodison Park because, by mid-January 1958, I hadn't kicked a first-team football for three and a half months. My last game for Hibs had been a 4-0 win over Airdrie at the end of September and now here I was in Liverpool, trying to contain players like Jimmy Murray of Wolves, Joe Hayes, my future team-mate at Manchester City, and 17-year-old Chelsea sensation Jimmy Greaves.

At this point, I was being firmly labelled in the newspapers and even in the match programme as a 'reserve team footballer', the only one in the Scotland side who wasn't playing regularly for their club. I was thinking about making a sign to hang round my neck. It was a bit of an unsettling period all round given that I was finishing up my joinery apprenticeship and would be joining the Army in just a couple of weeks. Getting the nod to face England again was a real shot in the arm and the rest of the lads were great. They didn't care if I wasn't playing for Hibs as long as I did my best for Scotland. I also got a bit of a pep talk from one of the selectors on the train down to Liverpool. 'Forget about the reserve label,' he told me. 'You're in the team because we feel you're the best young centre-half in Scotland. Go out and prove it.'

In what was fast becoming a tradition in this fixture, we had to put up with yet more fog, this time rolling in from the Mersey. Greaves, the teenager who had been taking the English First Division by storm, had also been in prolific form for the Under-23s, scoring four goals against Bulgaria and Romania in his first two games. It had taken him less than a minute to open the scoring against the Romanians, but it was our own in-form striker, Hearts' Alex Young, who gave us an early lead at Goodison, slipping the ball past Eddie Hopkinson after six minutes following a pass from Hearts team-mate George Thomson. We held firm for almost the whole of the first half until a sustained period of pressure just before the break saw Murray and then Greaves score twice in the space of three minutes. Hayes scored England's third from close range late in the second half.

We had been beaten and, within a couple of weeks, I had moved to Hampshire for my National Service. I still hadn't been able to regain my place in the Hibs team and, as such, the chances of being asked to represent my country again seemed remote. If someone had told me at that point that, within a year, I would be back in the Hibs line-up, play in a Scottish Cup Final, be made captain of the British Army team and then be chosen to captain Scotland's Under-23s against England, then I think they'd have heard me laughing all the way from Aldershot. But then it all just started to happen.

An injury got me back in the Hibs team to face Hearts in our memorable Scottish Cup win, I appeared in the final against Clyde and then I started playing for – and captaining – the British Army, which included a 6-1 drubbing of my own club at Easter Road. This, according to the newspapers, laid the foundations of the 'revenge duel' between me and Joe Baker. I was pleased to be named as a reserve for the Under-23 game with Wales in December 1958, but I was beside myself shortly afterwards to find out that, not only had I been chosen to play against the England Under-23s at the beginning of February, but I would also be captain. Joe, the Scotsman who would be leading the line for Young England for the third time, would be in direct competition with his Hibs team-mate – one who had managed to get the better of him a few months earlier. No wonder the sports reporters were sharpening their pencils in anticipation. Sadly, what was set to be easily one of the proudest moments of my career so far wasn't to be.

I'd already had one Under-23 cap against England taken away from me thanks to an icy surface and, just a day before the duel, I was robbed of another with Ibrox considered unplayable. I'd been denied again, this time as captain. If I ever bumped into Jack Frost in the mood I was in, the cheeky little sprite would have more than me nipping at his nose to worry about. I'd tried to compensate for the ice during the Easter Road trial match by tying bandages around my boots, but I'd have wrapped myself up like a bloody mummy if it meant the match going ahead. Joe would make his debut for the senior England team later in the year, but my wait for a full Scotland cap would continue.

I had been relishing the chance to follow in Dave Mackay's footsteps by captaining my country against England and I seemed to be inching closer to joining him in the senior ranks. It's always nice to feel wanted and, in early March 1959, I had three pieces of good news in one day. First, I found out I would be playing for the British Army against an Irish FA XI in Belfast on Wednesday 11 March 1959. Then I had to do a double take when I realised that, for the Scotland versus the Scottish Football League trial match the following Monday, I had been selected by both sides. I was in the starting line-up for the League XI and I was also named as the reserve for Bobby Evans, the Scotland captain, in the same match. It was explained to me that, in the event of Evans having to drop out, I would go into the Scotland team and my place in the League side would go to George McCallum of Third Lanark.

Now in its second year, the annual trial match was a good chance for the selectors to run the rule over players they were considering for the national team. And with Scotland facing England in the British Home Championships at Wembley the following month, there was all to play for. But just my luck, McCallum did indeed end up playing for the League XI, although it wasn't Bobby Evans who was on the sick list. After all the talk of me taking Evans's place should he be injured, I was the one who ended up missing the game after picking up a knock in a Scottish Cup defeat on the Saturday. And, just to keep piling on the irony, it was against McCallum's Third Lanark. Still, I thought, how memorable a match would I actually miss? The answer was emphatic – it finished 6-5 to the Scottish Football League.

I was still named as Scotland's reserve centre-half for Wembley, but, on the day of the big match, I was on league duty with Hibs, playing in front of 7,000 fans at Firhill. Bobby Evans, meanwhile, was representing Scotland in front of a near-100,000 crowd in London. As I said earlier, Bobby was a big hero of mine and even to be named as his back-up was an honour. England won 1-0 but I couldn't help wondering what it would have been like to play at Wembley in a match like that. I don't think Hibs would have had any qualms releasing me as the league campaign was all but over.

After missing out on the chance earlier in the year, I was delighted to be named captain of the Under-23s to face Wales in Wrexham in November. Dave Mackay was no longer eligible but we still had some marvellous players, including Duncan MacKay. The 22-year-old right-back was establishing himself at Celtic and represented the senior team against England back in April. And after playing with him at Under-14 level, I was reunited with debutant Adam Blacklaw in goal. Adam was in the midst of a championship-winning campaign with Burnley, but it was up front that we truly shone. Flanked by the Motherwell duo of Andy Weir and Billy Hunter, our men in the middle were Denis Law, then of Huddersfield, Alex Young, and John White, who had recently joined Spurs from Falkirk for £20,000. Looking at the three of them on paper now, it's a trio of talent that would be worth a fair amount in today's market – or any market, for that matter.

Several of Wales's team from the previous Under-23 international a year earlier could no longer be selected, including Charlton's Trevor Leonard, who was part of the 1958 World Cup squad. But they, too, had an impressive team, including Mike England, then of Blackburn but later of Spurs, and 18-year-old centre-forward Graham Moore of Cardiff City. Although this was his first appearance for the Under-23s, he had already played for Wales in two full internationals, scoring an 89th-minute equaliser against England just over a month earlier. It didn't get much better than that. We were also pleased to see Manchester United's Kenny Morgans playing at outside-right. As an 18-year-old, Kenny was the last survivor to be found in the wreckage in Munich when he was discovered unconscious by journalists five hours after the official search had been called off. And it was Kenny who put his side ahead after only 12 minutes in what was the first international match in Wales to be played under floodlights. There was a lot of mud and surface water from a downpour not long before kick-off, but Young equalised less than ten minutes later with a lovely flick from Weir's cross. Denis, always the focus of special attention from defenders, was getting a bit frustrated with a rather lenient referee, but he was more than capable of taking care of himself. The only player to go in the book was Young for retaliation. I felt we deserved to win, especially when White had a goal ruled out late on, but we couldn't be too disappointed with the draw, especially as Wales had won their two Under-23 internationals to date, against England and Scotland.

I didn't think I would have to move to England to finally win a full cap for Scotland but that's what happened, and it was in part due to an England centre-forward. In October 1960, one of Scotland's 'Big Seven' selectors was at White Hart Lane to watch Spurs play Manchester City. He wasn't there to see me, however. He was there to assess Denis Law as well as Tottenham's 'Anglos', Dave Mackay and John White. Spurs were going for their 11th league victory in a row and Bobby Smith, their big, burly number nine, already had 13 goals to his name. Although he did manage to score his 14th of the season against us, the fact that I was effectively able to 'blot him out' and help City become the first team to take a point off the eventual Double-winners hadn't gone unnoticed. Later in the month, Smith scored twice in England's 4-2 win over Spain and this helped tip the scales of selection in my favour when it came to choosing Scotland's centre-back against Northern Ireland.

Scotland rarely fielded the same team twice in those days, but my position had been filled consistently for many years, first by George Young and then by Bobby Evans. I had been named as Bobby's reserve on a few occasions but, by 1960, his time at both Celtic and for Scotland was coming to an end. Nearly 33 and no longer possessing the pace that had served him and Scotland so well over the course of 12 years and a then record 48 caps, the flame-haired number five had represented his country for the last time in a 4-2 defeat to Turkey back in June. The Celtic legend left Parkhead for an unhappy spell at Chelsea, finally leaving the door open for a new Scotland centre-half. For the British Home Championship match against Wales in October, that role went to John Martis of Motherwell.

It was suggested in the *Glasgow Herald* that, by fielding a young team against the Welsh, the SFA had one eye on the 1962 World Cup and, having not yet qualified for Chile, they were counting their chickens before they hatched. Cyril Horne wrote, 'There does not seem to be any point in concentrating on players young enough to be in the running for a place in the World Cup team proper before we concentrate on gaining a place in the competition proper.'

Indeed, after a 2-0 defeat in Cardiff, the selectors rang the changes against Northern Ireland, but it was still a side with youth in mind. Denis Law returned and three players were selected to make their debuts: me, Rangers striker Ralph Brand and his Ibrox team-mate, a 21-year-old left-half named Jim Baxter. Like me, Ralph would be too old for the Colts by the time their next fixture came around and, because players like Billy Hunter, Jimmy Gabriel, Ron Yeats – the reserve centre-half for the Northern Ireland match – and Ian Ure would be eligible for Under-23 duty for some time to come, the match at Hampden was a good chance to see how we fared.

We would be facing several members of the Northern Ireland team, which, like Wales, had reached the quarter-finals of the 1958 World Cup. These included Manchester United goalkeeper Harry Gregg, Spurs captain Danny Blanchflower, Celtic legend Bertie Peacock and Aston Villa outside-left Peter McParland, who scored five goals during their remarkable run to the last eight in Sweden. Nevertheless, Scotland had beaten them 4-0 in the corresponding fixture in 1959 and, to date, Northern Ireland had never won at Hampden. Significantly, the game in Belfast was also the last time that Scotland had beaten anybody, and they had now gone seven internationals without a win.

Following the resignation of Andy Beattie, the match would be Ian McColl's first as Scotland's new manager. The 33-year-old had only recently retired from a 15-year playing career at Ibrox and was another of the Rangers players that I had greatly admired as a youngster. Together with goalkeeper Bobby Brown, full-backs George Young and Jock Shaw, Willie Woodburn and Sammy Cox, 'The Iron Curtain' conceded less than a goal a game en route to the 1949 league title. Although this was his first managerial post, Ian had gained experience while acting as Scotland's player-assistant at the World Cup. He and I also had something in common in that he was part of the first Rangers team to compete in the European Cup in 1956/57. He still wasn't in charge of team selection. That wouldn't be the case until his former Rangers team-mate Bobby Brown took over in 1967. Indeed, in his first match in charge, he was described by one newspaper as a 'paid spectator', with McColl himself adding, 'What can you do with a team in an afternoon's training?' The answer, come the full-time whistle, was 'enough'.

Jock Stein had made a memorable comment about Old Firm supporters going to Scotland matches in the 1950s, saying that they 'went to internationals to cheer three players, boo two and ignore the rest'. If that was still the case in 1960 then it would have been nice to have a few more fans turn up to ignore me. Not helped by the driving rain, the number of people there to witness my Scotland debut was under 35,000 – around a third of the crowd that had watched Clyde beat Hibs on a previous visit to the national stadium. But as I stood in the tunnel, the only thing that truly mattered to me was that the moment I had been waiting for since I was a little boy had finally arrived. My heart beat faster as the thought sank in – I was about to follow in the footsteps of Willie Woodburn. I was going to play at centre-half for Scotland.

Denis – demonstrating why he was one of the finest headers of the ball I ever played with – gave Ian McColl a dream start after only nine minutes. After a few missed opportunities we doubled our lead just before half-time when our captain, Eric

Caldow, converted a softly awarded penalty. Unfortunately, it wasn't the only soft spot-kick English referee Kevin Howley decided to award. Three minutes after the break he penalised me for a tackle on Billy McAdams which everyone in dark blue thought was a: not a foul, and b: outside the box. Blanchflower didn't care, though, as he hammered the ball past Lawrie Leslie via the crossbar.

Jim Baxter impressed on his debut, forcing several good saves from Harry Gregg, but it stayed at 2-1 until 12 minutes to go when an Alex Young header kick-started a late flurry of goals. Brand opened his international account three minutes later, before McParland pulled one back with just a few minutes to go. Brand scored his second almost on the final whistle as we celebrated a 5-2 win, an identical scoreline to my first appearance in a Scotland Schoolboys shirt almost nine years earlier. After playing my part in an emphatic victory and, a soft penalty aside, not really putting a foot wrong, I thought I stood a good chance of staying in the team for the next match against England.

But a lot would happen before April 1961. Manchester City slid down the table, I lost my place in the side and I handed in a transfer request. I don't know how much that had to do with why I wasn't chosen to face England, but, even if my club fortunes had improved, the Scotland selectors clearly hadn't learned the value of keeping some level of consistency. After the team had recorded its first victory in over a year, four new caps were handed out at Wembley. At the time I was terribly disappointed not to have been picked but, in retrospect, if there was one game any Scotland player – or indeed, fan – would like to have missed, it would probably be the 9-3 defeat of 1961.

Bobby Smith, the man to whom I apparently owed my lone cap, scored twice. Scotland had used four different centre-backs in the space of four games. I was the only one to play on the winning side but, like John Martis, I was never selected to play for my country again. Had I been around today, when players can make two-minute cameos in seemingly endless qualifiers and friendlies, I might have clocked up a few more appearances, but caps were a little harder to come by back then.

Nevertheless, I couldn't really complain because my replacement was a fellow Bellshillian. And despite an international debut to forget against the English, 21-year-old Celtic defender Billy McNeill would win 29 caps for Scotland but, more significantly, become the first British player to lift the European Cup.

In 1963, when I was languishing in Manchester City's reserves, Scotland beat England 2-1 at Wembley. England captain Bobby Moore described the team that day as Scotland's finest. Looking today at the names in the visiting line-up, I'm reminded of that Eric Morecambe joke. I played with all the right players, just not necessarily in the right order. My Scotland cap remains my proudest possession and is on prominent display in my home. Yes, I'd have loved to have won another couple, but, when you consider that, out of the Famous Five, only Lawrie Reilly played more than 20 times for his country, then I should probably count my blessings. Turning out for Scotland was the highlight of my career, something that – by the time I turned 30 – I knew was effectively over.

14

A Former Player

THE WORKERS' hut stands empty, ready for the lunchtime rush. Save for the gentle hum of the tea urn in the corner – all is quiet. Suddenly, the silence is broken as a dozen men in heavy boots stomp inside like a herd of overall-wearing elephants.

There's laughter, there's micky-taking and, as always, there's talk of football.

Each of the men grabs a brew and then – other than the youngest, who has to perch on the edge of a rickety trestle table – each one then pulls up a chair. They open their bait boxes and hungrily dig into their sandwiches. Hard work in the fresh Scottish air will do that to you. Through mouthfuls of corned beef or cheese, they chat briefly about work before returning to more important matters.

'What do you think of Rangers' chances this season?' asks one of the men.

'Not much,' says another. 'I bet you this packet of biscuits that Celtic will win it again.'

'Don't forget Hibs,' adds a third. 'They're playing some great football at the moment.'

'Of course they are,' says a fourth member of the group, clearly a few years older than the rest. 'Eddie Turnbull's in charge.'

He shakes his head wistfully. 'Now he was a great player. So were the rest of the Famous Five.'

The young lad sitting on the trestle table decides to chip in. 'What's the Famous Five?' His footballing ignorance is rewarded with several dirty looks and a lump of pork pie is thrown in his direction. He returns sheepishly to his sandwich and the conversation continues.

'I bet you can't name the rest of the Famous Five,' says a man in blue overalls.

'Easy,' says his older colleague. 'Gordon Smith, Lawrie Reilly, erm...'

'Willie Ormond,' suggests one.

'And Bobby Johnstone,' says another.

'Oh aye, Bobby Johnstone. Didn't he go to Man City?'

I finally decide to pipe up.

'They had a centre-half that went to Man City too. I bet you can't name him.'

The older chap clearly knows his stuff. 'That's easy,' he smirks, before taking another swig of tea to buy a few more seconds' thinking time. 'Jackie Plenderleith. Decent player, Jackie. I don't know what happened to him, though.'

I smile and say, 'He's sitting here talking to you lot.'

It was probably the moustache that confused him, that and the setting. I didn't think I looked that different to how I did in my playing days, but my co-workers at that boat yard in Dunoon probably didn't expect to be sharing their lunch break with a former professional footballer. But that, unfortunately, was the reality for most of us once our playing days were over. And with many joining their clubs straight from school, it wasn't unusual to find footballers who had once entertained thousands of fans up and down the country now driving taxis, pushing trolleys or carrying hods.

From a financial point of view, there aren't many top-flight footballers these days who have to worry about what they're going to do next. If they aren't invited to offer their opinions on *Match of the Day*, on BT Sport or on Sky, they can always try their luck on the managerial merry-go-round. If none of these opportunities arise, then they can sink their millions into property or just go and retire to the Bahamas. Don't get me wrong, I've long made my peace with the fact that, from a financial point of view, I was born in the wrong era. And while I don't think there's any doubt that the pendulum has swung too far in the direction of players and their agents, I don't begrudge today's professional the rewards that me and so many of their predecessors were denied.

I was luckier than some in that I had listened to my dad's advice and learned a trade other than football. And it was this, too, that prompted my decision to come home from South Africa. I had been retained in October 1967 by Hellenic to play the following season but, almost immediately, I began to have second thoughts. With Mark now seven and Scott nearly five, their education was now front and centre of my mind. The question now was what to do when I got home.

For a boyhood Rangers fan, I thought my knight in shining armour had arrived in the unexpected guise of a former Celtic striker. Originally from Motherwell, Jim Conway was the youngest player to appear for the Hoops when he made his debut against Falkirk in 1957. After spells with Norwich, Southend and Partick, he joined Irish League side Portadown, becoming their player-manager in 1966. Jim was in negotiations with Hellenic for several months trying to bring me back to the British Isles, but the South African club wouldn't be budged. Portadown could have me but only for a price that they clearly couldn't afford. It was a bitter way to end what, for the most part, had been an enjoyable experience in Africa, but I had no choice but to see out my contract and we returned to Scotland in the autumn of 1968. We came back, once again, to where it all began, in Holytown. We moved in briefly with my parents – where I was reacquainted with my mum's delicious homemade soup – before getting our own house. I was able to find a job in a sports shop in Glasgow, but we didn't end up staying in Holytown for long. Anne got a job as a radiographer in Argyll, a position which came with a cottage in the grounds of the recently opened Dunoon and District General Hospital.

The Cowal Peninsula is one of the most beautiful parts of Scotland. Situated on the banks of the Firth of Clyde, Dunoon was once a popular seaside resort, especially for those Glaswegians who fancied a trip 'doon the watter'. Nevertheless, it was a bit far to commute to my job in Glasgow, so I did something that I'd fancied doing for a while – I opened up a sports shop of my own. I'd picked up a small amount of experience as a business owner back in my Hibs days, when I used to rent out a caravan, and felt that I could make a real success of it. I was genuinely excited when I opened the doors for the first time, especially when I saw my name in big letters on the sign. In retrospect, it might have fared better if I'd done what I did in South Africa and pretended that my name was Stanley Matthews!

But I think even the famous Wizard of the Dribble might have struggled to sell anything in Dunoon. Like most British seaside resorts, Dunoon's popularity had started to suffer in the 1960s with the advent of cheap foreign holidays. And following the controversial establishment of a United States nuclear submarine base at nearby Holy Loch in 1961, the town's demographic had also started to shift. With hundreds of American sailors and their families now living in the area, more baseball mitts and pigskins might have been in order.

It was after I closed up after a couple of years' trading that I was grateful to have had my training as a joiner, when I was taken on by the famous Alexander Robertson & Sons boatyard in Sandbank. Like the US submarine base, Sandbank sat on the banks of Holy Loch. The Firth of Clyde was hugely popular among yachters and had even hosted one of the sailing events at the 1908 Summer Olympics. Robertson's had an excellent reputation for its craftsmanship, designing and building yachts and smaller wooden vessels, including entrants in the America's Cup. Although the company was now under different ownership and now only made boats from fibre-reinforced plastic, there were still plenty of wooden yachts coming into the yard to be repaired.

It was a very satisfying job and all that time spent captaining football teams served me well when I was made a foreman. The last time I had worked as a joiner, I was just starting out on my football career and my hero Willie Woodburn stopped by to interview me. That felt like a lifetime ago and, although not sentimental, I was fast approaching my mid-30s and was beginning to miss the game. So I was delighted when, through a connection at the boatyard, I was approached about the possibility of coaching Dunoon Athletic, the local Junior side. Dunoon played in the Central League, competing mainly against teams from the Glasgow and Lanarkshire areas, including Bellshill. I was still fit and raring to go so it was too good an opportunity to turn down.

'I'll do more than manage you,' I told them, 'I'll play for you, too.'

The club was completely skint and, as a result, had a policy of relying on local amateurs rather than recruiting players from Glasgow or Edinburgh. I really enjoyed playing for Dunoon. They were a great bunch of lads who showed tremendous spirit, but we were never really in the hunt for honours and, having experienced it even at Junior level, I didn't really feel cut out for football management. I finally called time on my playing – and managing – days in the autumn of 1973, just before I turned 36. I might have carried on for a while longer, but the yard was taking up a lot of my time and I felt I couldn't really do both. Unfortunately the yard, which closed in 1980, was beginning to run into difficulties and I was soon forced to find another job.

It didn't take long before another exciting opportunity came my way, however, when Sir Robert McAlpine opened an oil rig construction yard at Ardyne Point. Located on Loch Striven, it was only ten miles from our home and one of several new yards in Scotland which aimed to capitalise on the North Sea oil boom. I didn't know anything about oil, but I knew a fair bit about joinery and I was part of the team that put together the wooden casing into which cement was poured during the construction of the enormous platforms. Over the next four years, three concrete gravity platforms were built at Ardyne Point, including the monstrous, 300,000-tonne Cormorant Alpha, which at the time was the largest oil production platform ever built.

What the job may have lacked in the romance of repairing yachts, it made up for in money, but this, too, came to an end with the closure of the site in 1978. Another chapter of my life was coming to an end in more ways than one. After 20 years of marriage Anne and I decided to go our separate ways and, hoping to continue working in the oil industry, I moved to Aberdeen in 1979. The job I had left in search of didn't materialise in the Granite City, but, scouring the recruitment pages of the *Press & Journal*, I found an advert for a position that would work out better than I could possibly have imagined.

I was working as a hospital porter in the early 1980s when I first met Susan. A group of us were out for some Friday night drinks and we got chatting. She was working part-time at the hospital and, like me, had been married before. We had a few things in common, including a fondness for animals, but football wasn't one of them. We started seeing each other, but she left the hospital shortly afterwards to get a full-time job with the city council. When she happened to mention that her partner's name was Jackie Plenderleith, the guys she worked with were really interested – at least those who were old enough to remember me. But as Susan is fond of pointing out, she had no idea I used to be a footballer when we first met and – given her complete lack of interest in the sport – she was equally unimpressed when she found out! That suited me – I had plenty of friends I could bore with my football chat – and Susan and I were married in Dunblane in 1993. By this time I had started working with the council as a gardener and became a supervisor before I retired. Today, we're still enjoying our quiet retirement in Aberdeen.

The city where I couldn't seem to buy a victory as a Hibs player has ended up being very good to me. After winning that memorable game against my Easter Road team-mates by finishing my round in the pouring rain, I still enjoy playing golf and I also like pottering around in the garden. But the aches and pains I sometimes get when teeing off or doing the weeding are a reminder that time can be unforgiving. I struggle to believe that it's been nearly 50 years since I last kicked a football and more than 60 years since I last wore a Hibs shirt. I find it harder still to believe that 70 years have passed since I turned out for Holytown in the final of the Airdrie Schools Cup, still one of my proudest days and one when I felt my whole life lay ahead of me. In August 2020, my eldest son Mark said he couldn't believe that he was turning 60. I just laughed and said, 'How do you think I feel? I've got a kid who's 60!'

I've got four grandchildren but, unfortunately, I don't get to see them as often as I would like. Scott's children, Lucy and Ewan, live in London, while Mark's two, Skye and Rhys, live in Australia. Ewan is an ardent Arsenal supporter. I don't think he believes me when I tell him that the Gunners once wanted to sign his granddad. Sometimes I'm not sure I can believe it either.

I still enjoy watching football on television, with Hibs winning the Scottish Cup in 2016 undoubtedly one of the highlights, but the game has changed massively since I last pulled on a pair of football boots. As far as football in Scotland is concerned, it saddens me that it's been more than 35 years since a team from outside Glasgow last won the league championship. Maybe I was spoilt as, from the time I first became properly involved in the game as a Scotland Schoolboys international, I watched the title go to seven different clubs in the space of 13 seasons. I think Rangers and Celtic would both benefit from a third or even a fourth horse entering the title race, but I just can't see it happening – not any time soon, anyway. The gulf between top and bottom seems to be greater than ever and, as for mega-rich Manchester City, it's unrecognisable compared to the club I was at for three seasons. Still, I don't think the blue half of Manchester will mind so long as they keep winning.

I loved being a footballer but retirement just creeps up on you and, like everything else in life, it's something that you don't fully appreciate until it's too late. The game had its frustrations, but it also gave me a lot of precious memories, many of which you've just read about. As you've probably gathered, I've nearly always been one for the quiet life and – the odd free entry into a music venue aside – never had any interest in being a celebrity. While not every aspect of my career turned out quite how I hoped it would, I'll always consider myself lucky that – having been in love with football since the day I learned to walk – I was in the right place at the right time when history came calling with Hibs and that I got to fulfil my boyhood dream of playing for my country.

One by one I've had to say goodbye to old team-mates, old rivals, old managers and old friends but, sadly, that's the way it goes. As for me, the game of life continues and – touch wood – I've managed to stay in reasonably good health. I've no idea when the full-time whistle is going to blow. There's no big electronic board to show me how much time will be added on for stoppages but, just like I did when I was on the football field, I intend to enjoy every last minute of it.

Epilogue

'LADIES AND gentlemen, we will shortly be arriving in Dusseldorf. Please return to your seats and make sure your seatbelts are securely fastened. Damen und Herren, wir werden in Kürze Ankommen …'

The soothing voice of the flight attendant wakes me from my daydream. I was looking absent-mindedly out of the window as Germany hove into view and, for a few moments, I was a 17-year-old on my first plane journey, heading out here for a date with footballing destiny. The aircraft was full of young players. Some were playing cards, others reading the newspaper and some chatting excitedly about the adventure that lay ahead and the prospect of meeting new opponents in a new competition.

The plane I'm in now is a lot quieter, a lot more comfortable and, best of all, I'm even able to enjoy a cup of tea and a Kit Kat. But that's not all that's changed. I glance across at my three travelling companions, who look resplendent in their green ties. Their hair – what's left of it – has turned grey, their faces are now lined and two of them are wearing glasses, but I would still recognise them anywhere: Lawrie Reilly, one of the greatest strikers British football has ever known, Tommy Preston and Jimmy 'Tiger' Thomson. The last time we made this journey together, Tommy, Jimmy and I formed the youngest half-back line in Scotland, but none of us are looking as young any more. That's because that journey – when we were all Hibs players – was 50 years ago. Lawrie agrees – he, too, can't believe that half a century has elapsed since that day.

It's July 2005 and we're flying to Germany as guests of Rot-Weiss Essen who, despite losing to us all those years ago, are still keen to mark what is a significant anniversary for both clubs. Bayern Munich, on several occasions, Hamburg and Essen's near neighbours, Borussia Dortmund, have all won club football's biggest prize since 1955, but nothing will ever change the fact that Rot-Weiss Essen were the first team from their country to compete in the European Cup. That's something that Hibs and Essen will always have in common.

These days, our German friends have an even greater reason to commemorate a time when they were national champions. No longer does the Red and Whites squad boast World Cup winners. They are now competing in the third tier of German football and the chances of playing in the Bundesliga again any time soon seem remote. Their amazing victory over FC Kaiserslautern in 1955 remains their only league championship and, like Hibs, the odds of winning another in the near future is unlikely.

When we arrive, we're treated to a traditional German welcome – a trip to the local brewery where we're told jokingly by Rolf Hempelmann, the Rot-Weiss Essen president, that tomorrow's pre-season friendly between our two clubs will be a chance to 'gain revenge' for 1955. For Tony Mowbray, the Hibs manager, the match has an added purpose. After finishing third the previous season, his side have qualified for the UEFA Cup, and facing old rivals Essen will be 'good preparation' for competing in Europe. 'The experience of playing against a German club in Germany will be good for the players,' he adds. 'The fact the match commemorates such an important landmark in the history of Hibernian Football Club makes it all the more special, especially for our fans.'

The following day, the late-July sunshine beats down on a lush, green surface which, the last time Hibs played here, was a sea of mud.

It may only be a pre-season friendly but there's a sea of red, white and green and a great atmosphere among the supporters in the Georg-Melches Stadion. In the match programme, the Hibs team of 1955 are described as 'Scottish Bravehearts' and, before kick-off, Lawrie, Tommy, Jimmy and I are invited on to the pitch to wave to the fans. None of us can believe that we're now standing on the same patch of grass where we played our first game in the European Cup 50 years earlier. It was also where we got covered in mud and where Lawrie scored one of his many superb goals. It's a special moment, although some of the younger fans who haven't been paying attention to the stadium announcements are probably confused as to why the cast of *Last of the Summer Wine* are doddering around in the centre circle. The four of us return to our seats and are pleased to see another Hibs victory, this time with Guillaume Beuzelin, Garry O'Connor and Gary Caldwell scoring the goals in a 3-0 win.

After the game, Tony Mowbray says, 'I was delighted for the older guys who played against Essen all those years ago and who made this trip. It was a very nostalgic night for them and I am pleased to have won for them as much as ourselves. For Hibs to have come here and won 4-0 in this environment is a pretty impressive performance but, as we all know, we had a pretty impressive team back then.'

Of that there is no doubt. Unfortunately for Mowbray, while his own side are able to gain experience of playing in Europe, it doesn't translate to the real thing. Two months later, they lose their opening UEFA Cup tie 5-1 on aggregate to Ukraine side Dnipro. For the 'older guys' in Essen, the wining and dining continues. At the reception afterwards we're even serenaded, if that's the right word, with bagpipes. A former member of the Rot-Weiss Essen coaching team tells us that, back in 1955, he couldn't believe the warmth with which the team were greeted during the return leg in Edinburgh, which included a tour of the sights of the Scottish capital. This evening, he said, was a chance to repay that hospitality. Memories continue to be shared and tokens of friendship are exchanged. Hibs present Herr Hempelmann with a set of engraved decanters, while the 'veterans' are each given a framed certificate to commemorate the occasion. Alongside my Scotland jersey, it still has pride of place in my home.

That reunion took place more than 16 years ago and, for obvious reasons, there won't be another. When I took the field against Rot-Weiss Essen I wasn't old enough to drink and, for me, it's a sobering thought that – since those wonderful 50th anniversary celebrations in Germany – Tommy, Jimmy and

Lawrie have all passed away. With this book, I'd like to raise a symbolic glass to all those I played with and against throughout my career, with an extra special 'cheers' to the rest of the history-making Hibs class of 1955.

Favourite European Moments

I USED to repair boats for a living, so I'm well acquainted with the adage, if it ain't broke, don't fix it. Unfortunately, just as they have done with their constant tinkering with the European Championships, UEFA have failed to heed that advice when it comes to the Champions League. And just like FIFA's approach to the international cash cow that is the World Cup, the never-ending desire to expand and to change the format has come at the cost of diluting the competition.

I know this will sound rich coming from someone who played in the tournament for a side which finished fifth in their domestic league, but I think the European Cup worked best as a straight knockout featuring only the national champions. Having said that, the Champions League has given us some incredible moments as you'll see below. It does worry me, however, that the growth of the competition hasn't only impacted the Champions League but also the domestic game. In England, for example, finishing fourth is seen as more important than winning the FA Cup, when the final at Wembley was once the most eagerly awaited day on the sporting calendar. Like countless others, I used to spend hours watching the build-up on television: the coaches arriving, the pitch inspections, even the God-awful songs were all part of the fun. Now the FA Cup Final is just one more game that's seen almost as an inconvenience to an ever-growing European schedule. And don't even get me started on teams being eliminated from the Champions League being allowed to drop into the Europa League, which must serve as the biggest slap in the face to those teams already taking part.

The Champions League format has now been fiddled with again and expanded by four teams. I don't know how this will pan out, but I do know that you can have too much of a good thing. You only need to look at what happened at UEFA's 2016 European Championships, when the competition was expanded to 24 teams – essentially half of Europe. When it's possible to escape from your group without winning a single game, it makes for some incredibly dull matches. Not that you heard Portugal complaining.

I just fear that, with more teams, the Champions League will become interminable and I must admit that I find myself caring less and less about who wins it. But enough of my grumpy old man act. I thought it would be nice to remember some of those amazing moments that the European Cup/Champions League has given us over the last 66 years. I'm not claiming this list is definitive; these just happen to be the goals and the matches that have stuck in my mind. It's not in any order and I certainly don't want anyone doing a Gérson and tearing it up in disgust like he did with Pelé's. Remember, we watch football for enjoyment – and those of us who were lucky enough to do so played the game for exactly the same reason.

The Miracle of Istanbul – 2005 final

Okay, so it's a predictable choice, but it's also one that's impossible to leave out. Every football fan loves a comeback, especially when it's their team that pulls it off, but, even for neutrals and for those who have little interest in the game this was a match that will never be forgotten.

In their first appearance in the final for 20 years, Liverpool were the underdogs against an AC Milan side boasting a galaxy of stars, including Cafu, Kaká, Andriy Shevchenko, Hernán Crespo, Andrea Pirlo and Clarence Seedorf. Then, of course, there was also Paolo Maldini, the 36-year-old captain who had been a titan in defence for club and country for nearly two decades. The writing seemed to be on the wall when Maldini fired Milan ahead after only 50 seconds, with Crespo adding two more before half-time. The amazing fightback began nine minutes into the second half when Liverpool captain Steven Gerrard powered in a header. Vladimir Šmicer scored a second from long range shortly afterwards and Xabi Alonso, following up his own saved penalty, snatched the equaliser. All three Liverpool goals arrived in the space of six breathtaking minutes.

After the drama of drawing level, there followed a tremendous backs-to-the-wall defensive display, including a terrific clearance off the line by Djimi Traoré and an amazing double save from Shevchenko by Jerzy Dudek. Afterwards, the goalkeeper was seen nodding and smiling as though to say, 'It's going to be our night, lads.' And after a triumphant penalty shoot-out it certainly was.

Matt Busby – 1968 final

It's still scarcely believable that ten years after being given the last rites in a German hospital, Matt Busby was celebrating winning the European Cup with Manchester United. It's even more amazing to think that two of the players who also survived the Munich air disaster – Bobby Charlton and Bill Foulkes – took part in the 1968 final against Benfica. Charlton scored two superb goals in the 4-1 victory, while George Best and Brian Kidd, who was celebrating his 19th birthday, got the others.

Scottish managers have made an indelible imprint on the English game over the years, but the first man to lead an English side to European glory will always be held in the highest esteem. I had recently begun my National Service when I heard about what had happened in Munich, when eight Busby Babes were among the 23 killed in a plane crash while returning from a successful European Cup quarter-final in Belgrade. What added to the shock for me was that, while playing for Hibs and for the Scotland Under-23s, I had come up against several of the players who had died. By the time Busby finally got his hands on the European Cup, my football career was over. Winning the trophy would never bring back the players he lost, but it did give the manager a sense of closure. 'When Bobby Charlton took the cup, it cleansed me,' he said later. 'It eased the pain of the guilt of going into Europe. It was my justification.'

Real Madrid – 1960 final

Did I ever tell you about the time I faced Ferenc Puskás twice in two days? Well, I'll not bore you with that fascinating fact again, but this final was one of the main reasons that playing in those two matches was among the highlights of my career. At this stage, there had only been one winner of the European Cup, with Real Madrid triumphing in the inaugural tournament – where this story began – and in the three competitions that followed. But securing a fifth in a row wasn't going to be easy.

Eintracht Frankfurt, their German opponents, were a good side. Just ask Rangers, who were swept aside 12-4 on aggregate in the semi-finals. Frankfurt's 6-3 second-leg win at Ibrox came less than two weeks before they returned to Glasgow for a much sterner test. Still, few among the 127,000-strong crowd or the 70 million watching on television could have predicted a 7-3 victory for Real – especially when Richard Kress had given Frankfurt an 18th-minute lead. Puskás scored four times, narrowly beating Alfredo di Stéfano – who scored the other three – to the first hat-trick in a European Cup Final. To this day, there has only been one other hat-trick in this fixture. The scorer? Ferenc Puskás, during Real's 5-3 defeat by Benfica in 1962.

But it's the 1960 showpiece that will live longer in the memory, as the one with the most goals, the largest attendance and a standard of entertainment that few finals have ever been able to match.

The Lisbon Lions – 1967 final

Even though I was a Rangers supporter when I was a boy, I wouldn't dream of missing out the first British team to win the European Cup on this list. Jock Stein was confident that his men would triumph in the 1967 final in Portugal, even against an Inter Milan side which had won back-to-back trophies in 1964 and 1965. History would show that the manager's confidence was more than justified.

It's a well-known fact that all bar two of that great Celtic team were born within ten miles of Parkhead, but it's a particular source of pride to me that nearly half the team were born in Lanarkshire. Bobby Murdoch hailed from Rutherglen, just south of Glasgow, while Tommy Gemmell, who scored the equaliser in Celtic's 2-1 win, was born in Motherwell. Jimmy 'Jinky' Johnstone, their dazzling outside-right, came from Viewpark and John Clark was born in Chapelhall. Both of these villages lie within three miles of where I grew up, in Holytown. Meanwhile, Billy McNeill, the captain and the first British player to lift the European Cup, was born in Bellshill – just like me and a certain Matt Busby. I told you there must be something in the water.

Ronaldo wows Juve – 2018 quarter-final

As the all-time top scorer in the Champions League, you might think it would be difficult to pick out one goal from the 130-plus that Cristiano Ronaldo has scored at this level. It's a phenomenal tally which includes four in the final itself. For me, though, it's an easy choice. Having already put Real Madrid a goal up after three minutes in the first leg of the 2018 quarter-final against Juventus, the 64th minute saw the prolific Portuguese produce an 'I was there' moment for the ages. With his back to goal, the Real number seven seemed to defy gravity when meeting Dani Carvajal's cross and scoring with one of the most picture-perfect overhead kicks ever seen. His team-mate, Gareth Bale, hit a spectacular effort in that year's final against Liverpool, but, for sheer aesthetic quality, I don't think I've ever seen a better overhead kick than Ronaldo's – and that includes Pelé's equaliser at the end of *Escape to Victory*.

What made the goal especially good was the way it left a goalkeeper of Gianluigi Buffon's quality rooted to the spot, while also causing Real manager Zinedine Zidane to rub his bald head in disbelief. But its true brilliance is marked by the fact that so many Juventus supporters, who had booed Ronaldo during the first half, stood up to applaud it – something that took even the notoriously humble Ronaldo by surprise. No wonder he ended up joining them.

Messi's magic – 2019 semi-final

I couldn't, in all good conscience, feature one of Ronaldo's finest moments without also including one from his great rival, Lionel Messi. Like Ronaldo, the Argentine has plenty of moments to choose from, including his goal in Barcelona's dominant victory over Manchester United in the 2011 final at Wembley. But like Ronaldo's goal against Juventus, I'm including Messi's magnificent free kick against Liverpool in the 2019 semi-final partly because of the reaction of others. In this case Jurgen Klopp, whose face mirrored that of football fans around the world.

When Messi's 35-yard free kick flew past Alisson in the 82nd minute, the Liverpool boss stood laughing in disbelief on the sidelines. Who in the world can produce that kind of a reaction from a manager whose team has just gone 3-0 down? I don't care if the ball took the slightest of deflections off Joe Gomez's shoulder in the Liverpool wall, this was an unforgettable moment of magic from one of the greatest players in history. The fact that it was also his 600th goal for the Spaniards was the icing on the cake. When that goal went in, very few would have predicted that Liverpool would go on to beat Barcelona 4-0 at Anfield and reach the final. Was nobody from Barcelona watching in 2005?

Picasso – 1980 final

John Robertson didn't look like a footballer. He smoked, he drank, he loved fried food and he was famously described by Brian Clough as 'a very unattractive young man'. The Nottingham Forest manager added, 'If one day I was feeling a bit off colour, I would sit next to him. I was bloody Errol Flynn compared to him. But give him a yard of grass and he was an artist. The Picasso of our game.'

Clough and his assistant Peter Taylor are rightly revered for what they achieved at Forest, winning the European Cup in 1979 and retaining the trophy a year later. But they wouldn't have done it without the Lanarkshire-born winger, a man who on more than one occasion has been voted by fans as the club's greatest-ever player. His dribble and cross set up Trevor Francis for the winning goal against Malmo in 1979 and, a year later, it was Robbo's turn. In the 20th minute against Hamburg, Robertson cut in from the left wing and played a one-two with a grounded Garry Birtles on the edge of the penalty area. Then, nicking the ball off the toe of Hamburg's Kevin Keegan, he arrowed a right-footed shot in off the post for the only goal of the game. 'You win something once and people say it is all down to luck,' said Clough later. 'You win it twice and it shuts the buggers up.' The genius of John Robertson certainly helped shut up a lot of those buggers with that goal.

Captain Keane – 1999 semi-final

We all know about the late drama of the 1999 Champions League Final in Barcelona, when injury-time goals from Teddy Sheringham and Ole Gunnar Solskjaer sank Bayern Munich and sealed the treble for Alex Ferguson's Manchester United. It was the ultimate demonstration of United's refusal to be beaten, but they might not have reached the final had it not been for the determination of their suspended captain.

Following a 1-1 draw in the first leg of the semi-final at Old Trafford, Juventus had the advantage when the second leg kicked off in Turin. But in the words of ITV commentator Clive Tyldesley, United were soon in need of a 'minor miracle' in order to progress. Within 11 minutes Juve striker Fillipo Inzaghi had scored twice and the dream of the treble had quickly turned into a nightmare. Enter Roy Keane. Although not renowned for his goals, the formidable Irishman had already scored twice in the competition and his textbook glancing header from David Beckham's corner in the 24th minute made United fans truly start to believe that this could be an historic year and they eventually won 3-2.

The other side of Keane's game was also on display that night, when he picked up his second yellow card of the tournament and was suspended for the final. What I found most impressive was the quiet dignity shown by him and Paul Scholes, who was also suspended, following the subsequent victory at the Nou Camp. Despite the immense contribution of both players in reaching that stage, both stayed mainly in the background and allowed those who had played against Bayern to enjoy the moment. It reminded me of Jimmy Greaves being forced to sit out the 1966 World Cup Final. He congratulated his team-mates and then disappeared into the crowd. Chelsea's John Terry, who famously changed into his kit – complete with shin guards – to lift the Champions League trophy in 2012, could have learned a lot from their example.

Ronaldinho – 2005 round of 16

With Lionel Messi and Cristiano Ronaldo dominating the headlines in recent years, it's easy to forget what an incredible talent Barcelona's brilliant Brazilian was. He won a Champions League medal against Arsenal in 2006, but it was in a last-16 defeat to Chelsea the previous season that he produced his most amazing moment in the competition. Barcelona had won the first leg 2-1 at the Nou Camp and the tie looked all but over when Chelsea raced into a three-goal lead within 20 minutes of the return leg at Stamford Bridge. That's when Ronaldinho took the tie by the scruff of the neck.

Just ten minutes after giving his side hope with a penalty, he received the ball on the edge of the area. Surrounded by blue shirts and with seemingly no options, the ball was suddenly in the back of the net. Chelsea goalkeeper Petr Cech was left standing still and wondering – just like the rest of us – how the world's best player had just done that. I remember being mesmerised watching the replay as, like a matador, Ronaldinho danced this way and that before sending a bullet-like toe poke past the bewildered Chelsea players and into the far corner.

The power and accuracy of the shot was matched only by its artistry. A second-half header from John Terry settled the tie, but it's a measure of Ronaldinho's genius that – even after such an incredible victory for Chelsea – it's the Brazilian maestro's goal that's still being talked about.

Zidane's volley – 2002 final

I genuinely don't think there has been a better goal to win a Champions League Final, or possibly a final of any kind. Real Madrid, aiming for their ninth triumph, had reached this stage of the competition for an incredible 12th time. Bayer Leverkusen, who had knocked out Manchester United in the semi-finals, had reached their first final and had no intention of making it easy for the Spaniards. Raul had put Madrid into an early lead only for Lúcio, Leverkusen's Brazilian centre-back, to head an equaliser. Then, on the stroke of half-time, came one of the greatest moments in the history of the competition.

Another Brazilian, Real's Roberto Carlos, sent over a high, looping cross from the left to Zinedine Zidane, who was waiting just inside the area. Few players in the world would even have attempted a volley like that, but with a graceful swing of his left foot, the Frenchman sent a beautiful, unstoppable shot into the Leverkusen net. Iker Casillas, Real's young substitute goalkeeper, made a series of excellent saves towards the end of the match, ensuring that Zidane's strike was the worthiest of winning goals. The fact the match took place at Hampden Park, 42 years after Real had wowed supporters with the victory over Eintracht Frankfurt, made it all the more fitting.

Acknowledgements:

Anne Baillie

Maurice Dougan

Fred Eyre

Laura Hopcroft

David Litster

Janice Macgregor

Fordyce Maxwell

Jenna Maxwell

Iain McCartney

Chris McGinley

Robert Plenderleith

Susan Plenderleith

Barry Sullivan

Bibliography

Eyre, Fred: *Kicked into Touch* (Senior Publications, 1981)

Fabian, A.H. and Green, Geoffrey (editors): *Association Football, Volume Two* (Caxon Publishing, 1960)

Ferguson, Ronald: *Black Diamonds and the Blue Brazil* (Northern Books, 1993)

Litster, John: *A Record of Post-War Scottish League Players 1946/47 to 2017/18* (*Scottish Football Historian* magazine, www.scotlandsfootballers.com)

Maxwell, Tom: *The Fabulous Baker Boys – The Greatest Strikers Scotland Never Had* (Birlinn, 2013)

Reilly, Lawrie: *The Life and Times of Last Minute Reilly* (Black & White Publishing, 2010)

Scott, Brian: *The Terrible Trio* (Sportsprint Publishing, 1990)

St John, Ian: *The Saint – My Autobiography* (Hodder & Stoughton, 2005)

Turnbull, Eddie: *Having a Ball* (Mainstream Publishing, 2006)

Other publications:

Cape Argus, The Courier, Daily Express, Daily Herald, Daily Mail, Daily Mirror, Daily Record, Dumfries and Galloway Standard, Evening Citizen, Edinburgh Evening News, Glasgow Evening

BIBLIOGRAPHY

Times, The Guardian, The Herald, Liverpool Echo, Manchester Evening News, Motherwell Times, The People, Rand Daily Mail, The Scotsman, Sunday Mirror, Sunday Post, Wishaw Press

Websites:

bbc.co.uk, bluemoonmcfc.co.uk, britishpathe.com, englandfootballonline.com, englandstats.com, fitbastats. com, manutd.com, qosfc.com, realmadrid.com, rsssf.com, scotlandfootballstats.co.uk, scottishfa.co.uk, secretscotland. org.uk, thecelticwiki.com, thestatcat.co.uk, uefa.com